CLEAR

YOUR

MENTAL CLUTTER

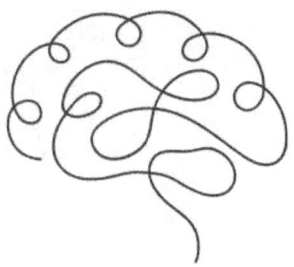

Calm Your Busy Mind, and Replace Worry with Peace
Mindful Habits & Exercises to Stop Overthinking

BY AMELIA SAGEWOOD

For permission requests or inquiries, contact:
The Awesome Readers

www.theawesomereaders.com

Print ISBN: 979-8-9926575-0-0

Hardback ISBN: 979-8-9926575-1-7

ABOUT THE AUTHOR

Amelia Sagewood is dedicated to helping people create balance, clarity, and calm in their daily lives. With a focus on practical strategies for decluttering both the mind and the home, she empowers readers to simplify their routines, reduce stress, and embrace a more intentional lifestyle.

Her books combine gentle guidance with actionable steps, offering readers the tools they need to let go of overwhelm and make space for what truly matters. Whether it's clearing mental clutter or creating a peaceful home environment, Amelia's mission is to inspire lasting change through simplicity and mindfulness.

When she isn't writing, Amelia enjoys quiet mornings with a good book, long walks in nature, and the simple joy of an organized, peaceful space.

YOUR EXCLUSIVE ACCESS

Thanks a million for being here. Your support means so much to me!

The best way to keep in touch with me is by signing up for my newsletter –
https://theawesomereaders.com/

Or scan the QR Code below

See you soon,

Amelia Sagewood

TABLE OF CONTENTS

ABOUT THE AUTHOR 3

PART I: GETTING ORIENTED 1

CHAPTER 1: INTRODUCTION 2

CHAPTER 2: WHO OR WHAT IS LIVING RENT-FREE IN YOUR HEAD? 4

The Uninvited Guests in Your Headspace.. 5

Catching the Thought Loops on Repeat – Because Not Everything Deserves a Rewind................. 7

Modern Life: The Ultimate Brain Clutter Machine.. 9

Wrapping It Up: Your Mental Declutterb Masterpiece.. 11

PART II: LETTING GO OF WHAT DOESN'T SERVE YOU 12

CHAPTER 3: THE POWER OF EMBRACING YOUR IMPERFECTION 13

Counting the Costs of Perfectionism.. 14

The Easy Way to Stop Being So Hard on Yourself... 16

Turning Your Imperfections into a Superpower.. 19

Finding Calm Amidst the Chaos.. 21

CHAPTER 4: LET IT GO (WITHOUT LOSING YOUR SANITY): DECLUTTERING LIKE A PRO 23

The Subtle Art of Keeping Your Cool.. 24

Putting the Calm into Your Daily Chaos.. 26

The Mind-Protecting Power of "No"... 28

From Mental Burnout to Mental Balance.. 30

CHAPTER 5: YOUR BRAIN REAL ESTATE: WHAT'S WORTH THE RENT?... **31**

Keeping Your Life Under Control..*32*

Dream Big, but Nap Sometimes..*34*

Stop What You're Doing and Start Prioritizing......................................*36*

Wrap Up...*37*

PART III: BUILDING MENTAL STRENGTH **39**

CHAPTER 6: DIGITAL DETOX: THE ART OF SHUTTING DOWN YOUR MENTAL OVERLOAD **40**

Uncovering the Sneaky Tech Habits That Destroy the Peace..................*41*

Mastering the Art of Tech-Free Time...*43*

Multitasking: When Doing It All Means Doing Nothing Well.................*44*

Ditch the Pressure, Keep Your Peace...*46*

CHAPTER 7: MINDFULNESS FOR THE REAL WORLD **48**

Gratitude Is the Power Move That Sets You Free...................................*49*

Do One Thing Well and Ditch the Circus Act..*51*

Making Mindfulness a Daily Habit..*53*

Mindfulness Is Peace by Design: Building a Life That Actually Feels Good.........*55*

CHAPTER 8: HOW SMALL CHANGES IN YOUR MIND LEAD TO BIG WINS **57**

Your Brain Loves a Good Workout...*58*

Feeding Your Brain the Good Stuff, Not the Junk.................................*59*

Recharge Your Mind By Sleeping Your Way to Calm.............................*61*

Your Daily Dose of Wellness..*62*

PART IV: RESILIENCE AND JOY **64**

CHAPTER 9: WHEN LIFE BURNS, BRING SOME BANTER!...........**65**

From Panic Attacks to Laugh Attacks: How Humor Melts Stress...........*66*

The Neuroscience of Lols: Comedy as Cognitive Nutrition....................*67*

Turning Your To-Do List into a Lol List..69

Life's A Joke, So Laugh It Off...71

CHAPTER 10: SMASH THAT RESET BUTTON AND GIGGLE YOUR WAY FORWARD 73

Your Strategy Playbook for Quick Wins in Everyday Life.................................74

The Mind Workout For a Lifetime of Calm...75

Daily Laughs to Lighten Your Load..77

The Never-Ending Quest to Clear Your Mental Space.......................................79

PART V: WRAP-UP 81

CHAPTER 11: STEPPING RIGHT INTO THE SHAMBLES! 82

The "Messy Room" Metaphor..83

Untangling the Mental Mess: What's in Your Head?..85

Stress Management 101: Laugh It Away...87

Wrapping It Up: Insights, Giggles, and a Pinch Of Sass................................... 90

REFERENCE LIST 93

PART I:
GETTING ORIENTED

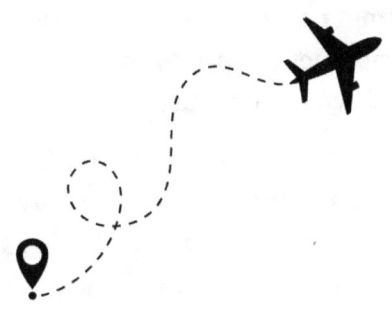

CHAPTER 1: INTRODUCTION

Clear Your Mental Clutter: Calm Your Busy Mind, and Replace Worry with Peace Mindful Habits & Exercises to Stop Overthinking

We've all been there. You walk into a messy room and immediately want to turn around and walk back out. You know your eyes is already on the exit as you deem that to be the wise things to do in such a scenario. What you may not know is, our brains work pretty similar. Our mind sometimes can be a busy melting pot of to-dos, occasional intrusive thoughts, overthinking, responsibilities (especially in young adults) and other things that bog the mind of an active individual.

But this book isn't to teach you to become some Zen meditation master or to write gratitude lists in a leather-bound journal every morning. It's about helping you navigate the mental maze with a mix of humor, relatable advice, and tried-and-true strategies that've helped people over the years. See it as somewhat as your handy guide for a much-needed brain detox. Here, you'll find practical tips to simplify your thought process, amusing moments to lighten your mood, and strategies to deal with stress that don't involve completely losing it. So, if you're stuck overanalyzing everything, trying to juggle multiple items, or just wondering why your brain feels like a bustling airport terminal during holiday seasons (with announcements blaring in peak rush hour!), then you'll find this book incredibly helpful.

Who's This Book For?

To put it simply, this book is for you if:

1. You're a young adult who feels like life is a stuck on the hamster wheel and is seeking an exit strategy.

2. You're a college student trying to balance deadlines, social life, and the all-too-familiar existential crisis that pops up at 2 a.m.

3. You've ever searched for your phone while it was literally in your hand. lol.

If your brain won't stop buzzing and you're ready to finally close the open tabs in your brain, then this book should be your new best friend.

Why Read This Book?

Very quickly, you'll learn you're not the only one struggling to keep it all together. Because life's way too short to feel like your brain is stuck in overdrive, we'll show you some clever techniques to help clear out the clutter, tame the chaos, and make some mental space for what really matters.

CHAPTER 2:
WHO OR WHAT IS LIVING
RENT-FREE IN YOUR HEAD?

Ever felt like your brain is hosting its own 24/7 radio station—but instead of playing your favorite hits, it's stuck on static, old jingles, and that one embarrassing memory from middle school? That's mental clutter, my friend, and in this chapter, you'll learn that it's time to hit the reset button on your brain's chaos playlist.

Think of this chapter as your flashlight in a dark mental wilderness, helping you shine a light on what's crowding your head and why it's so dang hard to focus sometimes. There are a number of factors that may create a mind miss in our minds. On certain days, it could be self-criticism turning every tiny mistake into something worse that affects your self-confidence. On other days, its you overcommitting to the point where you're stretched. Whatever it is, we'll dive in to figure out where these cluttered thoughts come from, and how they take up residence in our mental real estate.

We'll also unpack the greatest hits of mental clutter triggers: past experiences that show up like uninvited guests, fears of the future, and our modern lifestyle that's basically a buzzing hive of notifications, expectations, and a caffeine overdose. By the time we're done, you'll have a clear map of these mental landmines and some strategies to dodge them like the ninja of self-awareness you're about to become.

You'll learn to say "no" without spiraling into guilt. You'll also learn to embrace uncertainty, with the kind of optimism usually reserved for puppies. This chapter is all about making space in your brain for things that actually matter. Overall, you'll learn everything you need to keep your mind sharp and clear the way for peace, focus, and maybe even a little joy. So, grab your imaginary brooms, because it's time for some housekeeping!

THE UNINVITED GUESTS IN YOUR HEADSPACE

Every so often your brain moonlight as a mean-spirited sports commentator. Every little mistake made gets a play-by-play breakdown, complete with slow-motion replays and sarcastic commentary. This is your inner critic, and boy, does it love to turn up the volume. It'll take what could've been a helpful nudge (like, "Hey, maybe don't send that email without proofreading") and morphs it into full-blown mental clutter. To avoid landing into trouble, you may need to learn how to differentiate between constructive feedback and destructive noise. Unfortunately, this is a delicate balancing act for most. But once you can nail this sweet spot, we can describe the benefits as tuning out the static of a radio - once you tune out the static, you can finally enjoy the music. In the saw way, knowing when self-criticism goes off the rails can be empowering, as it gives you the power to hit mutse on that inner heckler and start moving forward instead of spiraling into chaos.

Overcommitment is another way you can take control internally to bring about positive outward change. Overcommitment is the act of biting off more than your brain can chew. It can feel like juggling a dozen flaming torches, only to end up getting third-degree burns instead of applause. Here, the pressure to do all the things is less about productivity and more about creating chaos. Newsflash: it's okay to say "no." In fact, it's practically a superpower. Research by Weigelt et al., 2023, found that when we overcommit, burnout, fatigue, remains inevitable. This is why learning to say "no" gracefully can be the simple but effective tool to help you reclaim your time, energy, and sanity. All in all, every time you decline something unnecessary, you're basically saying "yes" to the balance, clarity, and presence of mind you need to think clearly and move closer to your life goals and ambitions.

There have been past experiences that you've tried to erase from your memory for years, but they have a way of sneaking into your thoughts uninvited, stirring up doubt and regret, and essentially pulling you back when you should be on the move. When this happens, you can control your memory to keep only what brings joy while letting go of the rest. It starts with taking a moment to sort through those mental keepsake. Learn from the ones that still hold value and toss the rest into the recycling bin of your mind. It is true that discarding memories is not always possible, and trying too hard may push painful truths underground when they should be healed. But this is where courage comes in. It takes courage to confront the past, and once you do, you'll feel like you've cleared out prime real estate in your brain for better, brighter things.

Meanwhile, let's not forget the biggest challenge of all – the fear of the unknown. The fear of the future looms large on most of us - like a storm cloud hovering over us, ready to rain on our parade and soak us in anxiety. But what if you flipped the script? What if you saw life as one of those "choose your own adventure" books where you never know what's on the next page, but that's about half the fun? Embracing uncertainty can actually make you more resilient to curveballs thrown your way. It's like planting the seeds of growth in a garden, one where you can't fully predict its outcome but you know will bloom. Kyron et al., 2021, even highlights how adapting to life's curveballs is essential for mental health. And this rings true whether you're taking baby steps or making big leaps. Facing the unknown with curiosity instead of fear will help you as you coast through life because you will find that most roadblocks are in fact, a stepping stone.

So, don't be afraid to tune out your inner critic and say "no" to the circus act of overcommitment, tackle those pesky past shadows, and welcome the mystery of what's next.

CATCHING THE THOUGHT LOOPS ON REPEAT – BECAUSE NOT EVERYTHING DESERVES A REWIND

Sometimes, our experiences have a way of dictating our moods in an unhealthy way. And the concept of "thought loops" exemplify this. Thought loops are an ugly occurrence where your brain feeds on a recurring mental playlist of negative emotions – regrets about mistakes, worries, or ideas that keep circling back in your head. Spotting these patterns can be tough. It's a bit like shining a flashlight into the creepy basement of your mind—it might be a little uncomfortable at first, but once you see what's lurking, you can finally start a proper cleanse.

Take this example: You're always panicked about failing exams. The basis for this fear is not necessarily valid. It could be for a reason as flimsy as you bombing a spelling test back in fifth grade. Thought loops cage you with that notion, and by spotting this, you can finally face the fear instead of letting it hijack your mental focus on the task at hand.

To engineer your thoughts in this manner, you have to start by becoming a detective of your own brain. Grab your magnifying glass and start tracing the events leading up to when those worrisome thoughts go into overdrive. You may want to write them down, too. The gist is to take stock. Once they're finally on paper, they magically shrink from "terrifying" to "manageable." It is at that point you begin to probe why these worries keep showing up uninvited. Ask yourself: Is there something you've been avoiding? (Spoiler alert: there probably is.)

Avoidance thoughts is are another critical mental loop that leads to serious brain clutter. Also known as procrastination. When we procrastinate, we dodge things that are important to us until they become impossible to ignore. Avoidance thoughts are like shoving everything into your closet before company comes over. While it sure feels satisfying in the moment, the penny drops eventually, the coffee gets cold, and chaos sets in when fast approaching the deadline, or upon seeing that a deadline has lapsed. You may put off that biology assignment or tough conversation with a colleague and it feels easier in the short term, but it creates mental clutter later on.

The trick is to 'catch' yourself in the act of avoidance. Ask yourself: "Am I skipping this because it's not worth my time, or am I skipping this because I am scared to deal with it?" If it's fear, divide the task into bite-sized pieces, or just a long timer and challenge yourself to focus for just that task. You'll be surprised how much progress you can make with a little structure (and maybe some coffee to keep the flame of your progress burning)

Perhaps the most consequential mental clutter to an individual is negative self-talk. You know, those doubtful little voices ping-ponging in your head that underrates and underestimates your ability at every turn. "Why even bother? You're going to fail anyway." The truth is, most of us will need to suppress these thoughts to progress in life. And if we fail in suppressing it, take action anyways. Successful people, for this reason, would swear by the art of "doing it afraid"; "doing it uncertain"; "doing it anyway".

But if left unchecked, we risk allowing this voice to become the soundtrack of your life, and let it dictate our affairs. Want to fix it? Keep a thought journal to log every time your inner critic makes an appearance. You want to be watchful: Observe patterns, identify moments. Then, you can start rewriting your script. Turn your negative self-doubt into positive, empowering mantras that you tell yourself a thousand times over until it becomes your reality. When you sow these motivational seeds in your mental garden, you will inevitably reap a lush jungle of self-confidence.

Between social media, endless notifications, and group chats the keep dinging our cell phones, a multiple things are pulling us hither and thither, so it can be a bit difficult not to get distracted. Alas, it is important to note that distractions is one of the ways to quickly rack up mental clutter.

How can we come unstack? Start by figuring out your main triggers. Is it Instagram? TikTok? That one YouTube channel with videos you swear you'll just watch "for five minutes" and end up watching "till mama calls"? Once you've identified your weak spots, implement some guardrails to help you control access or time spent on these habits. You could set limits on screen time, use apps to block distracting sites, or schedule designated breaks for indulging in your favorite digital vices. The only way to tackle distractions is to reclaim your focus. Only then can you free up mental space for what truly matters.

Each of these thought patterns contributes to mental clutter in its own weird, annoying way. But the good news? Once you spot the patterns, you can start trashing them. This head-on approach will leave you with a clearer focus and calmer mind. Remember, it's all about playing offense instead of defense with your brain. And if life has taught us anything, it's this: It's a game worth winning.

MODERN LIFE: THE ULTIMATE BRAIN CLUTTER MACHINE

Today's world feels like trying to juggle flaming swords while riding a unicycle. In other words, it's a lot. Inundated by constant notifications, breaking news, and social media updates flying at you like dodgeballs, our brain tends to run on smokes every so often. This concept, known as "information overload," is basically your mind yelling, "ENOUGH ALREADY!"

Considering this, how do you free up space? Curating your information sources consciously is a good place to start. Choose only the good stuff – what genuinely adds value and make you feel informed without the side order of existential dread. Eliminate the fluff. Unsubscribe from clickbait chaos, and simply let your brain breathe a little. In this moment, you want to prioritize quality over quantity. (Hampton et al., 2015)

Now let's talk about the ultimate frenemy, Social Media. While it keeps us connected, it's also the hot bet for comparison culture. We all can attest to this: Scrolling through a perfectly curated Instagram highlight or reel could leave you feeling like you're the only one not living your best life. Well, we're not sure if you know this, but nobody's life is really that perfect - not even that influencer who somehow makes avocado toast look like it's a new culinary discovery.

A digital detox has been reported to tackle most of the mental drawbacks of excessive social media consumption. At the very least, a digital declutter may be enough. Go through your feed and unfollow or mute any accounts that make you feel like you're not enough. Replace them with people or pages that make you laugh, inspire you, or remind you that it's okay to wear sweatpants three days in a row. Let your online space feel like a safe space. Not a high-pressure social environment.

And then there's the busyness trap. In our hustle culture, being constantly "on" has become some weird badge of honor. But let's be real: running at full speed all the time doesn't make you a productivity guru—it makes you a car about to run out of gas. If you ignore that little fuel light, thinking, "I'll just keep going," you'll eventually sputter to a stop and end up stranded on the side of the road with zero energy and a lot of regret.

The solution? Chill out. Seriously. Take breaks. It could be as little as a five-minute meditation, or a Netflix binge. You could even stare at the ceiling while questioning your life choices (don't worry, we won't judge you). These little pauses act as a refueling stop for your brain to help you recharge and come back to life's tasks with fresh energy, and a renew focus.

The loneliness curveball is a contributing factor to mental clutter, and it's not hard to see why a lot of people overlook this. Remote work and digital hangouts have made it possible to communicate 24/7. Yet somehow, we've never felt more disconnected. It may be a good time to go analog. Meet up with friends in real life, rather than a your daily slack huddle. Join a local club, or awkwardly wave at your neighbor and maybe strike up a conversation. Human connection isn't just nice, we need it for our mental wellbeing. In-person moments give you the kind of emotional depth emojis and virtual connection just can't capture.

To stay sane in this digital age, you need to strike a healthy balance. Embrace the tech, but don't let it rule your life. Set boundaries, take breaks, and remember: being constantly "on" doesn't mean you're truly living. Sometimes, the best moments happen in the quiet, when you unplug, slow down, and finally give yourself permission to just be . (The Impact of Social Media on Mental Health | PepTalk, 2024)

WRAPPING IT UP: YOUR MENTAL DECLUTTERB MASTERPIECE

Throughout this chapter, we've taken a deep dive into the wild, messy jungle of mental clutter—and what a ride it's been! From those inner critics who sound like the world's worst motivational speakers ("You're going to fail, but nice try!") to the chaos of juggling too many tasks at once (hello, multitasking burnout), we've unpacked some of the biggest culprits that tangle up your thoughts. The good news? This mental traffic jam you're experiencing can go away when you simply recognize these patterns. When you do, you can start peeling back the layers to untangle the mess.

We've also talked about the sneaky ways past experiences, fear of the future, avoidance, and distractions add to the mental clutter pile. We know how these things tend to take up residence in the nooks and crannies of ours mind. But identifying and dealing with them will give our brain a much-needed spring cleaning.

When this is done, you make space for good tidings and positive energy - joy, peace, clarity, you know, basically all the things your inner critic lied to you about being too busy to enjoy. So, we recommend that you take these insights and start building your path to a clearer, calmer mind. Remember, all the small, tiny steps you're taking add up. After all, Rome wasn't decluttered in a day. lol.

PART II:
LETTING GO OF WHAT DOESN'T SERVE YOU

CHAPTER 3:
THE POWER OF EMBRACING
YOUR IMPERFECTION

In many ways, we can compare perfectionism to shiny Instagram filter everyone loves. Sure, it might look great at first, but not managed properly, it could turn your life into an exhausting, anxiety-filled field of unfulfilled expectations. Of course, aiming for greatness sounds noble, but when you're stuck trying to make *everything* perfect 24/7, it starts to feel less like ambition and more like dooming yourself to a life of round-the-clock pressure, especially when it doesn't need to be that way. If it wasn't already obvious, living in this mental state is not sustainable. And In this chapter, we'll dive into some of the sneaky ways perfectionism messes with your creativity, joy, and overall chill. Life doesn't always fit into neat little boxes, and honestly? That's what makes it fun.

Now, here something to note: Striving for perfection often does more harm than good. Setting impossible standards doesn't just stress you out; it turns even small wins into "not good enough" moments. It's just like you're running a marathon and beating your personal best records in the process, only to complain eventually that you didn't win the whole race. You see, perfection isn't some ticket to happiness or success. When you are immersed in perfectionism, you're on the express lane to burnout. And the worst part? It doesn't just mess with your head; it can also strain your relationships. Nobody wants to hang out with someone who needs every game night to run like a military operation.

Perfectionism also traps you in a teeny-tiny comfort zone you're too scared to leave. Trying something new? Well, maybe it gets too risky. A slim chance of it ending up in potential failure? No thanks. Before you know it, you're stuck in a cycle of sameness, clutching your A+ track record while secretly dying to try something messy and fun, like pottery or karaoke.

Now let's tackle stress. Whether it's school, work, or planning the "perfect" party, perfectionism is the ultimate energy thief. It piles on pressure, drains your motivation, and turns minor hiccups into full-blown disasters. Wrinkled shirt? Yep, your brain thinks it's the apocalypse.

But it almost always isn't this way. And there is a way to unstuck yourself from this self-limiting mindset. Throughout this chapter, we'll share stories and insights to help you spot the perfectionist trap and climb out of it. You'll learn how to embrace imperfections and focus on realistic goals that build confidence, and a vital sense of security you need to forge ahead in your life. The truth is, life's messy, and that's what makes it worth living. So, let's ditch the tightrope act and start building a path that's balanced, fulfilling, and maybe even fun. Perfection? Overrated. Progress? Now that's more like it!

COUNTING THE COSTS OF PERFECTIONISM

Perfectionism might sound like the superhero of personality traits. Always striving to do your best, never settling for mediocrity. But when this "superpower" turns into an obsessive quest for flawlessness, it's role in your life becomes less of a "hero" and more of a "villain." Let's say you're chasing after an ideal so impossible it might as well involve you living on the moon, and no matter what you achieve, your inner critic is like, "I'm not doing enough." This is the joyless hamster wheel of perfectionism! Studies even show that this relentless cycle isn't just exhausting; it's linked to anxiety, depression, and even suicidal thoughts (Sandoiu, 2018). This tells you one thing: Perfectionism is not the glorified virtue you probably once thought it was.

Perhaps the worst attribute of perfectionism is its ability to paralyze you with fear. The second you're faced with the possibility of a mistake, you panic. Instead of taking a risk, you stay in your comfort zone, and as we all know, in this place, nothing exciting ever happens. Sure, it's cozy, but it's also boring and filled with missed opportunities. That pottery class you wanted to try? Not today, because, heaven forbids your first mug looks more like a lopsided pancake. Perfectionism keeps you stuck, holding you back from growth and new experiences because you're too scared to 'mess up'.

As a student, perfectionism can be especially burdensome. The pressure to ace every test, nail every project, and somehow also have a social life can quickly become a recipe for burnout. You sacrifice sleep, mental health, and probably a few friendships on the alter of having a perfect academic record. The irony to this is that burnout tanks your productivity, leaving you too exhausted to do anything, let alone achieve perfection. It's the hamster wheel all over again, but this time the hamster's given up and taken a nap.

Beyond messing with your head, perfectionism can mess with your relationships too. When you expect others to live up to your impossibly high standards, it's a recipe for frustration. Your friends might feel judged when they don't meet your expectations, (and a lot of times they won't) and this will create tension. Over time, those closest to you might start pulling away, leaving you with fewer relationships and even more time to perfect that to-do list.

Our harshest critic is the voice one inside our head. This relentless inner voice is always there to remind us that we're not good enough, no matter how much you accomplish. Most of the time, this is not true, and this voice is usually rooted in our quest for perfection. Just landed an amazing internship? "Sure, you did OK, but you didn't get that other one." Cooked a delicious dinner? "Well, could've used more salt." This constant stream of negativity is exhausting, chipping away at your self-esteem over time in a way that will leave you stuck in a cycle of self-criticism. (Nazari, 2022)

As if that weren't enough, it also takes a toll on your body. Medically speaking, the chronic stress of trying to be flawless has been linked to health issues, like high blood pressure, and cardiovascular problems. Turns out, striving for perfection can literally be bad for your heart. And if you do get sick? Perfectionists tend to struggle more than others, placing even more stress on themselves to "cope perfectly." Studies even suggest that perfectionism can predict early death for those with chronic conditions because of the relentless pressure they put on themselves (Sandoiu, 2018). Yikes.

The social media frenzy has proven to worsen the perfectionism problem. We see this in girls especially, where constant scrolling through picture-perfect feeds can fan the flames of self-critical thoughts. Everyone's life looks flawless online, and it's easy to start comparing yourself to highlight reels, leaving you feeling inadequate. It's like playing a rigged game where everyone else seems to have cheat codes for glowing skin, dreamy vacations, and perfect avocado toast (Nazari, 2022).

But the bottom line is this: Perfectionism is more than just a quirky personality trait. A perfectionist mind is a full-on villain wreaking havoc on your mental health, relationships, and personal growth. But recognizing it is the first step to kicking it to the curb. When you embrace your imperfections, you're not necessarily giving up on your success or lowering your standards; you're basically choosing progress over perfection and giving yourself the grace to be human. Because, think of it: isn't life a lot more fun when you're not chasing moon-level ideals?

THE EASY WAY TO STOP BEING SO HARD ON YOURSELF

If you want to break free from perfectionist tendencies, you have to unlearn a few things. If this were a journey, when packing, you start by ditching the "just in case" extras and realizing you don't need five pairs of shoes for a weekend. It's about shedding enough mental baggage that may possibly distract from any real progress that could be made in your life. It's a journey filled with challenges, rewards, and cringy moments where you realize how paradoxically self-limiting the obsession to the perfect can be. The first step? Setting realistic goals. Yes, realistic goals. Not those sky-high, "reach for the stars or bust" goals that leave you questioning your life choices. Many of us grew up believing anything less than perfect was failure (thanks, pop quizzes and overly enthusiastic coaches), but guess what? That's a lie.

Setting achievable goals means you're not giving up on ambition, but ditching the unnecessary pressure. If you were to take on a project and focusing on getting it done well, rather than obsessing over every tiny detail, like whether your PowerPoint transitions impress enough, you may well stay stuck looking for the right slide when you would have made significant progress in other areas that may contribute to a more compelling presentation. The gist is clear. By shifting your expectations from "perfect" to "very good," you'll not only stay motivated but also start enjoying the process. When you embrace the idea that mistakes are part of learning, you are more empowered to follow through with the process and get it over the finish line with stories to tell about your experience. You then realize that dropping an egg while cooking just makes for a funny story later.

Having self-compassion is another way to defeat perfectionism. Now, I know what you're thinking: "Compassion for myself? That's just an excuse to slack off!" Nope. Self-compassion isn't about slacking. It's being kind to yourself when things don't go perfectly. Think of it as being the friend who says, "Hey, it's okay, you're doing your best," instead of the one who yells, "Why didn't you fix this sooner?!" Perfectionists do well with self-criticism, so adopting self-compassion is like reprogramming your inner voice to be less of a bully and more of an empowering friend.

To tap into the power of self-compassion, you can write positive affirmations. Statements like "I'm allowed to make mistakes" or "I am enough even if my cookies turn out looking like pancakes." Repeat these truths until they stick. Over time, you'll stop beating yourself up over every tiny misstep and start realizing that even when you stumble, you're still moving forward. Nobody's perfect, and honestly, life's a lot more fun when you're okay with being a little messy.

Now, let's talk about *Comparisonitis* - the chronic need to measure yourself against everyone else, especially on social media. Scrolling through highlight reels of people living their best lives (or pretending to) can be exhausting, unproductive, and totally unnecessary. Instead, focus on your own progress. When you catch yourself thinking, "Wow, they're so much more put-together than I am," take a minute to reflect on how far *you've* come. Celebrate your own little, unique wins - even if it's just managing to wake up on time or finally folding that mountain of laundry.

Are you ready to shake things up? If you are, then try experimenting with imperfection. Yeap, you read right. Do something knowing it won't be perfect. Pick up painting and embrace the fact that your "tree" might look like a green blob, or cook a meal knowing full well it could end up being a burnt offering to the kitchen gods. The point isn't to succeed; it's to let go of the pressure and have some fun. You'll be surprised how liberating it can be to let imperfection run the show for a while. Who knows? You might even discover a hidden talent or, at the very least, make some hilarious memories.

Ultimately, don't forget that these changes take time. Perfectionism is a habit, and like all habits, it didn't take form overnight. As a result, it may not vanish overnight. Start small. Swap out a few unrealistic goals for more meaningful and achievable goals. Practice kinder self-talk. Celebrate every little win, no matter how tiny it feels. Progress isn't about reaching the finish line in record time; it's about learning to enjoy the ride, potholes and all.

So, set achievable goals, be gentle with yourself, ditch comparisons, and welcome imperfection. The road to freedom from perfectionism is messy—but honestly, that's what makes it so great.

TURNING YOUR IMPERFECTIONS INTO SUPERPOWER

Life can be beautifully messy, and honestly, that is its charm. When you embrace life's perfect imperfections, you realize that all of a sudden, the chaos in your kitchen mid-baking experiment isn't the disaster you previously made it out to be—it's just flour art and creative chaos. Think of it: Batter splattered on your shirt, flour on the dog, and somehow, amidst the mayhem, you're laughing, learning, and maybe even making something edible. Life can be like that, a deliciously messy recipe full of unexpected flavors and lessons.

So when you celebrate these flaws, you take ownership of your story. You turn those "oops" moments into growth opportunities. And let's be real, sometimes we as humans tend to gloss over the opportunity for human bonding that imperfections present. Here's the kicker: nobody bonds over perfection. You don't look at someone's flawless Instagram post and think, "Wow, we're so alike!" Nope. It's the friend who shares their speech-gone-wrong or the project that flopped that makes you go, "Ouhhh, been there, too." Our imperfections are what connect us; what reminds us that nobody's life is spotless, even if their social media feed says otherwise. Sharing your misadventures is like giving others permission to exhale and say, "Phew, me too."

This explains why chasing flawless achievements can be the ultimate trap. Perfection is like a finish line that keeps moving, no matter how close you get. So what if, instead, you celebrated the effort? Remember the first time you rode a bike? It wasn't glamorous. There were wobbles, maybe a scraped knee, but each awkward attempt brought you closer to cruising. That journey, the dedication, persistence, and the result of staying the course even through all of the slip ups. This is the stuff of magic. It's where the magic happens. When you shift your focus from "flawless results" to "look at me trying my best," life feels a lot more satisfying, and way less stressful.

Mindfulness is another way to savor the glorious unpredictability of life. It's being fully present in the moment, even when it's messy. Take that rainy picnic that turned into a spontaneous dance party. Sure, it wasn't in the plan, but it became a memory you'll never forget. Mindfulness lets you soak in the little details. The sound of rain, the smell of wet grass, the squelch of your muddy shoes, without worrying about how it "should" have gone. When you're present, even the hiccups in life become highlights.

And this brings us to your vulnerability, a trait people mistake to be a weakness. Vulnerability is your superpower. Brené Brown (the queen of vulnerability wisdom) reminds us that being open and honest is what builds genuine connections (Vijeth, 2023). Letting people see the real, messy you creates trust and deepens relationships. Think about the friend who sat with you during a rough time; it wasn't their Hallmark-worthy pep talk that mattered. It was their willingness to be there, unfiltered, and empathetic. Being   vulnerable doesn't just strengthen friendships; it invites new ones by showing people they're welcome to be real with you, too.

The best part? That you embrace life's messiness doesn't mean you have to lower your standards. What it means is that you've ditched the unrealistic pressure to have everything figured out from the get-go. Being young adults and college students, it's easy to feel like you're supposed to be nailing every aspect of life, but to be honest, this is not how it plays out in real life. So staying vulnerable through your flaws whilst celebrating your stumbles will help you stay grounded, balanced, and sane.

Life's isn't a tale of perfectly aligned stitches; it's the crooked threads, colorful knots, and unexpected patterns that make it interesting and uniquely your story to tell. Your imperfections aren't flaws. These are what have made you the person you are. They are opportunities for personal growth, deeper connections, and reminders to laugh along the way. So, embrace the mess, lean into the chaos, and never forget that life's best moments are rarely perfect. Although, they're forever worth it.

FINDING CALM AMIDST THE CHAOS

Having ripped off perfectionism's shiny mask and exposed it for what it really is: a joy-sucking, progress-blocking, mental health nightmare, we progress in this chapter to show you proven tips and tricks to help you keep your calm. This is important because striving for "perfect" can keep us stuck, thanks to constant self-doubt and the crippling fear of failure. For young adults and college students trying to juggle life, grades, and the occasional social life, this pressure can me more of an hindrance than the enabling mindset you truly need to perform well. If it wasn't already obvious, real progress doesn't require perfection. In fact, it thrives on imperfection. All of the world's most impactful innovations were a product of different trials and errors. These iterations could have been classified as failures in their own rights. But because these founders resisted the urge to cave into such self-limiting thoughts, they were able to advance and open themselves to blind spots and opportunities for improvement that led to their breakthrough. Not to get too motivational here, but the point is clear: the moment you realize that a little messiness isn't a roadblock but a stepping stone, things start to click. By understanding how perfectionist tendencies mess with your mental health, strain your relationships, and drain the fun out of life, you're already taking the first step toward breaking free.

So, what should be your game plan for ditching perfectionism? It's not as simple as pushing a button inside of your head. Remember we talked about setting realistic goals? Yeah, those ones that don't make you want to cry every time you look at your to-do list? Good. You should focus on that. Next, harness the power of self-compassion. Self-compassion is basically giving yourself the grace to be human (and thus prone to errors) rather than kick yourself every time you made a mistake and expect to be some flawless robot (unrelated, but even Robots like Gen-AI tend to make the odd error, a concept called AI hallucination). And then there's the idea of trying new things just for the joy of it, without worrying if you'll be good at them. Looking to paint a masterpiece that looks more like fingerpainting? By all means, go for it. It's the effort, not the outcome, that counts.

To completely fix the mental element and remove roadblocks that help you stay focused, do well to shut out the endless comparisons on social media. Scrolling through everyone else's highlight reels does you absolutely no favors. Your worth isn't tied to how picture-perfect your avocado toast looks compared to someone else's. Plus, your peace of mind is way cooler than chasing likes and online validation.

As you will sometimes find, life is messy. It's a glorious (sometimes chaotic) cocktail of quirks, stumbles, and surprises where each misstep is just another chapter in the hilarious, unpredictable story of being human. So, embrace the mishaps, laugh at yourself, and any time you're faced with your imperfections, try to remember that growth doesn't come from nailing everything. It's from showing up, trying your best, and learning from whatever crazy, unexpected curveballs life throws your way.

CHAPTER 4:
LET IT GO (WITHOUT LOSING YOUR SANITY): DECLUTTERING LIKE A PRO

Whether addictions or sticky thoughts, letting go to declutter your mind can be incredibly tasking. But it's an art form, and it gets easier when we view it that way. There is a way to manage the need to let go without waving the white flag and giving up entirely.

Ready to let go? Let this chapter is your ultimate guide to wrangling the thought tornado in your head. In this section, we'll explore proven techniques to help you let go of thoughts, notions, and negative self-talk that are not serving you like a hot potato – all while preserving your precious little sanity!

Mindfulness and meditation form the two basic pillars of mental decluttering, and each of these practices will be instrumental to your bid to release yourself from mental strongholds. These practices are like hitting your brain's "refresh" button, helping you quiet the constant mental chatter. Some of them highly recommended and we discuss them in this text. If you're thinking we're not about to tell you to sit cross-legged on a mountain for hours, well, we're not. Don't fret. Instead, prepare to get practical, actionable exercises that even the busiest, most stressed-out person can fit into their day.

From simple breathing exercises you can do between classes (or during awkward silences) to more structured meditation techniques, this chapter will arm you with tools to tackle your mental clutter head-on. You'll learn how to weave these practices into your daily routines. With these tips, you'll turn mundane moments (e.g., waiting in line for coffee) into valuable opportunities to breathe, reset, and maybe even feel like you've got it together (even if you don't!).

So buckle up, because you're about to embark on a journey of self-discovery that's equal parts calming and empowering. By the end, you'll be a master of letting go, with a healthier mindset and enough mental clarity to finally cruise through life. Let's do this.

THE SUBTLE ART OF KEEPING YOUR COOL

Now let's be real here. Mindfulness and meditation might sound like things your friend who wears yoga pants 24/7 keeps raving about, but don't roll your eyes just yet. Beyond trendy buzzwords, they are OG mental detox tools that have helped people declutter their brains for centuries. It's the ultimate sorting chamber for your mind, a mechanism that puts you in a position to keep the good stuff and let go of all that unnecessary junk.

Now let's break it down for a sec. Picture your life as a backpack filled with random stuff: old receipts, vintage watches, tangled earbuds, maybe even a rogue French fry (we won't judge). Over time, it gets so heavy and chaotic that you can't find anything useful, even if there were things you would ordinarily find useful in that bag. That's the effect of your brain on clutter. Mindfulness helps you dump the whole thing out and sort through it. What do you actually need? What's just weighing you down?

In a nutshell, being mindful means focusing on what's happening right now instead of obsessing over the past or freaking out about the future. It's basically a reset button for your brain. (Hoshaw, 2022)

The best part? Mindfulness is absurdly simple. No fancy gadgets, no "journey to the mountaintop" required. You can do it while sipping coffee, brushing your teeth, or pretending to pay attention in a meeting. It's all about anchoring yourself to the moment, which, in a world of constant notifications and never-ending group chats, is like unlocking a secret superpower. (Murphy, 2024)

Once you've dipped your toes into mindfulness, you might want to upgrade to meditation to take things up a notch. Meditation is like taking your mental fitness to the next level. If mindfulness is a casual jog, meditation is the gym workout that turns your brain into a finely tuned machine. There are so many styles to choose from, and you're bound to find one that fits your vibe. Want structure? Try guided meditation. Prefer something more chill? Body scans will let you mentally wander through every inch of your body, noticing sensations without judgment.

But this is not to say that meditation is a silver bullet. It's more like learning to ride a bike. On the way, you're going to wobble, fall, and maybe even get frustrated. There will be hiccups occasionally, but with mastery, it becomes second nature. The benefits tell the same story every time: they are worth it. Regular meditation can boost your concentration and help you adapt to life's curveballs like a pro.

But it gets even cooler. Science says meditation can actually change your brain. Yep, we're talking about boosting gray matter and improving emotional regulation like some kind of mental superhero. Studies even suggest it slows brain aging, which means fewer "senior moments" in the future. So, if you've been feeling frazzled or scattered, a few minutes of meditation might just be your secret weapon. (Murphy, 2024)

Knowing the theory is one thing, but putting it into practice? That's where it gets tricky. Start tiny—like, literally two minutes tiny. Find a snug spot where no one will bother you, set a timer, and just focus on your breath. Simple, right? Some days, your mind will feel like a hyperactive monkey swinging through the trees, and that's totally normal. Meditation isn't about getting it perfect; it's about showing up and giving it a try (Murphy, 2024).

Feeling restless? Bored? Ready to yeet the whole idea? Don't give up— switch things up instead. Try a new meditation app, join an online group, or experiment with different techniques. Variety keeps it interesting and helps you find what works for you, whether it's loving-kindness meditation or just sitting quietly and pretending you're on a tropical beach.

Beyond personal growth, mindfulness and meditation can level up your relationships too. When you listen mindfully, you're actually present —no zoning out, no scrolling through your phone. This kind of focus reduces misunderstandings and makes people feel genuinely heard. Imagine having conversations when you both walk away feeling like rockstars. That's the power of mindfulness: cutting through the noise and creating stronger, more meaningful connections.

So, there you have it—mindfulness and meditation aren't just good for your head; they're game-changers for your life. Try it out, stick with it, and watch your mental clutter fade into oblivion.

PUTTING THE CALM INTO YOUR DAILY CHAOS

In today's world, balancing is much of a delicate balancing act. Chaos has become the norm. But there's nothing to worry about if you make sure to imbibe mindfulness and meditation into your routine. You can think of them of that tiny little voice in your head that holds your hand and speaks clarity to you in the dark. You'll be surprised how well these simple practices can bring some tranquility into your daily madness.

You want to start by taking a deep breath. No, seriously, do it right now. Inhale deeply, then feel your lungs do their thing. Afterwards, slowly exhale. Done? Congratulations! Now, you've just completed step one of mindfulness. You've hit the reset button on your brain, so whenever you feel like your thoughts are 'doing the Macarena', all you need is a few conscious breaths to ground you and help clear out mental clutter (Pal et al., 2018). Bonus: it's free, requires zero equipment. The best bit? You can do it literally anywhere (except maybe underwater, for obvious reasons!)

Carving out a little meditation nook in your life will have the effect of a VIP lounge for your brain. You don't need much - it could be a corner in your room, a bench in the park, or even that one chair nobody uses in the living room. Here, the point is to create a space you can meditate regularly. You's want to treat it like brushing your teeth or your morning coffee. Basically, a daily ritual you can't skip. Keep at it and before you know it, this meditation corner will become your personal sanctuary where you swap chaos for calm. Who know? Maybe you'll even start looking forward to those few peaceful sessions each day. In any case, one thing you want to be is to be consistent. , and having a set spot for this ritual makes it way easier to build this habit (5 Simple Ways to Practice Mindfulness in Daily Life, n.d.).

If the idea of sitting quietly and meditating feels overwhelming, don't panic—there's an app for that. In fact, there are so many apps for that. Tools like Headspace or Calm will do well to guide you through meditation sessions with the soothing voices of people who sound like they've never stressed about anything, ever. You'll get everything from beginner-friendly breathing exercises to advanced techniques. Plus, a cheerful notification reminding you to meditate is a lot better than your usual "Pay Your Bills" alerts. These apps make meditation accessible, structured, and even kind of fun (Pal et al., 2018).

Let's talk about another overlooked mindfulness gem: mindful listening. Imagine you're in a conversation and actually listening —not just nodding while planning your next witty comeback or checking Instagram under the table. Wild, right? When you listen mindfully, you're fully present, phone tucked away, and genuinely paying attention. This will prove a game-changer for your relationships. It'll make conversations deeper, connections stronger, and everyone involved in your life feel like they matter. What's more, it helps cut through the noise of daily life and limits feelings of self-doubt in your thoughts and speech.

Perhaps the greatest hurdle to implementing this practice is actually remembering to do it. Life is busy, and remember, habits don't build themselves. But then, tiny drops of water make a mighty ocean. They key is to start small. Even if just a few minutes a day. Set reminders on your phone, slap sticky notes around the house, or tell your roommate to yell

"BREATHE!" at you occasionally. Morning stretches are another smart way to add a quick breathing exercise. If you're scrolling TikTok before bed, swap five minutes for meditation. Remember, it doesn't have to be perfect, it just needs to be consistent (5 Simple Ways to Practice Mindfulness in Daily Life, n.d.).

Of course, things will not always go smoothly. On some days, you'll sit down to meditate and realize your brain is playing a highlight reel of some of your most cringe-worthy moments from middle school. Or maybe you'll forget to practice altogether because life happens. But that's okay, too. Afterall, mindfulness isn't about perfection. It's about showing up and trying. Celebrate the small wins, stay focused, and don't be shy about getting some help. Friends who can keep you accountable will be very helpful in your journey. Meditate together, laugh about the silly moments when one of you falls asleep mid-session. The point is to make mindfulness and meditation feel doable and fun, not some item to check out on your to-do list.

In starting this journey, you must remember to give yourself grace. It doesn't matter if you're meditating for five seconds or five minutes. Every moment spent practicing builds on your depth of inner peace. Make mindfulness your secret weapon against life's noise and watch yourself attain the highest peak for yourself.

THE MIND-PROTECTING POWER OF "NO"

In an increasingly cluttered world, mental minimalism can be the detox we all didn't know we needed. With mental minimalism, you want to keep only thoughts that spark joy (or, you know, are actually useful) and toss the rest into the mental donation bin.

To start you can think of your brain like a messy junk drawer. You know, the one brimming with old batteries, random receipts, and that one key you're scared to thrash just in case it's important. Ask yourself: what's necessary, and what's just clutter? You must prioritize the thoughts and tasks that truly matter. Once you trim the excess, you'll be amazed at how much more mental clarity and energy you're able to channel into what truly matters in your life.

You also wan to set boundaries. Boundaries are not just walls to keep stuff out. They're portals that allow what serves you and politely shuts out what doesn't. Saying "no" is your way of protecting your mental faculty from being overrun by overcommitment. For a young adult juggling work, relationships, and TikTok scrolling, boundaries are the secret weapon against burnout. Plus, when you say no to draining activities, you're actually saying yes to things that align with your values, goals, and rest which we need to bring our A-game.

Admittedly, it can be difficult, but the trick is to shift your perspective. When you refuse to give in to the 'guilt' of seeming like a bad person, you'll take meaningful steps towards mastering your time, energy, and self-respect.

Simple strategies are always a good place to start. Blocking out time each week for quiet reflection (and yes, that means no phones) can bring you closer to mental clarity. Also, take an inventory of stressors you can eliminate, excess commitments, or even the physical stuff, like decluttering your physical space or simplifying your wardrobe. The gist here is "less is more". This applies to everything from your closet to your social media habits. And make no mistake: The minimalist mindset isn't about cutting all the fun out of life. It's consciously choosing what deserves your focus. Flooded with invitations? Pick those that feed your soul or align with your ambitions. Say yes to things that matter and no to everything else without feeling guilty. Every yes must be a step toward who you want to become, not just a way to be busy.

Finally, keep track. Every so often, step back, assess, and realign with your goals. Are you still on track? Do you need to make adjustments? This regular tune-up ensures your brain runs smoothly and is equipped to handle life's twists and turns with ease.

FROM MENTAL BURNOUT TO MENTAL BALANCE

We get it: starting new habits can feel like trying to teach a cat to fetch. It might be frustrating, but not impossible. The key is to stay patient and, most importantly, have fun with it. There are different meditation apps to help with this. You can also loop in a friend to share your progress (and laugh about how bad you both are at sitting still).

If your mind starts wandering mid-meditation or you skip a session because Netflix is calling, then know that it happens to the best of us. However, let one thought guide you: Every mindful moment is like adding to your mental piggy bank, building up a reservoir of calm for scenarios when you need it the most. So, dive into mindfulness, giggle at the awkward starts, and celebrate the tiny victories along the way. After all, it's not just about finding clarity, it's also about enjoying the ride there, one mindful session at a time.

CHAPTER 5:
YOUR BRAIN REAL ESTATE:
WHAT'S WORTH THE RENT?

Prioritization is basically the art of deciding which tasks deserve priority in our brain's limited real estate and which ones can wait in line (or, to be fair, get kicked out entirely). In a world where your to-do list multiply like recurring decimals, it's easy to feel like you're stuck in an hamster's wheel of stressful scenarios, infinite deadlines, and forgetful moments. Suppose you're lugging around a massive backpack filled with rocks, one for every task you've agreed to take on. It's definitely not fun, right? But if you're tossing out the rocks you don't actually need, your load becomes lighter. Now, you're no longer questioning every life decision that led you to this point. That, friends, is the magic of prioritization: ditching the unnecessary stuff so you can focus on what really matters.

In this chapter, we'll have a proper look at the concept of prioritization, starting with the Eisenhower Matrix, which is basically the 'Swiss Army knife' of strategies for taming chaos. You'll learn how to tell the difference between tasks that crave your attention but don't matter in the long run, and those quiet little to-dos that are more about building your future. Prioritization means separating the "fire drills" from the "chill drills." And so we'll help break down the eternal battle of urgency vs. importance to help you map out your responsibilities with a clear head.

We're also going to explore the incredible power of saying "no." Seriously, the word "no "is a superpower that cuts down your stress levels simply by not taking on every random request that lands in your inbox. By learning to say "no" to what doesn't serve you, you'll keep your plate from being unnecessarily overflowing and impossible to manage.

As you get to read on, you'll see how the tiniest, little shifts in your priorities can create massive changes and create less stress, fewer meltdowns, and more time for the things you actually enjoy. You'll discover practical tips and relatable insights that helps you to manage life's demands with structure.

Get ready to transform how you tackle your everyday chaos, as this chapter arms you with tools, tricks, and maybe even a laugh or two to help you create a harmonious balance between crushing your goals and taking care of yourself. Let's dive in!

KEEPING YOUR LIFE UNDER CONTROL

Balancing school, work, and a social life can feel worryingly overwhelming. And the initial idea of prioritization sorting this out for good can often seem about as real as unicorns or finding free parking downtown. But prioritization is not only real, but it's also surprisingly manageable when you've got the right tool, the Eisenhower Matrix.

So, what is this magical tool that promises to bring some calm to your chaotic schedule? The Eisenhower Matrix is basically your new bestie for task management. It's like sorting through the noise to figure out what actually matters and what's just pretending to be important. Picture it as your personal sorting chambers where you get to group your to-dos based on urgency and importance. It helps you stop wasting time on distractions and start focusing on the stuff that makes a real difference (Asana, 2024; Scroggs, 2021).

Here's the gist. Not all tasks screaming "NOW!" deserve your attention. Some urgent tasks will make your brain yell, "Do this or else!." Typical scenarios of these kinds of tasks include submitting an assignment due tomorrow or responding to a text from your boss. Important tasks, though, are the quiet, meaningful ones that build your future, like learning new skills, working on a passion project, or building solid relationships. It is helpful to know the difference between these two, because then, you can stop letting the urgent stuff run your life and start steering the ship of your life in the right direction. (Asana, 2024).

The magic is simple. Draw a square, split it into four sections, and there you go! Each box is a different category:

- **Handle first (urgent & important):** Take care of this now before life throws a tantrum.

- **Plan it (important but not urgent):** Schedule it without panicking—future-you has it under control.

- **Pass it on (urgent but not important):** Let someone else take the wheel (delegation is a superpower).

- **Cut it out (neither urgent nor important):** That third binge of your favorite show? Not happening.

Just putting tasks into these neat little boxes feels like tidying the junk drawer in your brain. Suddenly, chaos is under control, clarity emerges, and maybe you even feel a spark of joy (Asana, 2024; Scroggs, 2021).

Suppose your life is a hot mess right now - You've got this big essay due, your room looks like a tornado hit it, and somewhere in between you promised your friend you'd grab coffee. Here's how the matrix saves the day:

- Essay? *Handle first.*

- Messy room? *Schedule it.*

- Coffee with your friend? Move it to future-you.

- Netflix binge? Into the *Cut-It-Out box*—no regrets.

The beauty of the matrix lies in its flexibility. As life's realities change, so will your priorities. When exam season hits, your quadrants will probably need a major remix to make room for study sessions, panic, and the odd snack break. The trick is adjusting your matrix as you go, keeping your priorities in check while balancing productivity with self-care (Scroggs, 2021).

It's not just about managing your own chaos, either. Example - you're part of a team planning a massive campus event. There are a million moving parts, from sending invites to booking venues to figuring out who's bringing snacks. In such a case, the matrix can help you and your team sort through the madness, assign tasks, and actually stick to a timeline. Suddenly, the impossible feels doable, and everyone stops running around like headless chickens. You'll go from stressed-out event planner to teamwork champion, all thanks to this little framework (Asana, 2024; Scroggs, 2021).

If life feels like a runaway circus, grab the Eisenhower Matrix and reclaim your sanity. It's simple, surprisingly effective, and might just save your mental space—one quadrant at a time.

DREAM BIG, BUT NAP SOMETIMES

Today's fast-paced world can quickly feel like life is one giant tug-of-war—school deadlines yanking on one side, social obligations pulling on the other, and somewhere in the middle, you're just trying not to faceplant. The secret to not completely losing your mind is to figure out what deserves a spot on your brain's VIP list. With that being said, how can you decide what's worth your precious mental bandwidth? Let's break it down.

First, take a deep breath and assess your current chaos. Conduct an inventory of your life. Are you juggling way too many things? More importantly, do all these things actually spark joy (or at least serve a purpose)? If not, let some stuff go. Treat your commitments like your closet: keep the essentials and toss the stuff that's just taking up space.

Once you've decluttered your schedule, then map out a plan. Enter SMART goals—the gold standard for turning your vague "I should probably do this" into a clear, actionable roadmap. You've probably heard it before: Specific, Measurable, Achievable, Relevant, and Time-bound. Think of SMART goals as drawing yourself a treasure map. Instead of saying, "I should study more," say, "I'll study two chapters of biology every Tuesday and Thursday evening." This brings you instant clarity on what your goals are, and what you should be doing to hit your goals. As you check off each chapter, you get that sweet hit of satisfaction, like leveling up in a video game, which helps you stay motivated.

Perhaps the hardest life skill (which you will need in plentiful doses) is the fine art of saying no. Sounds easy, right? Two letters. N-O. No. But if you've ever found yourself as the go-to person for every group project, favor, or random task, you know saying no can feel like delivering bad news to someone who probably didn't deserve it. But let one thing be clear: Saying no isn't about being mean— it's about protecting your sanity. Every time someone asks for your time, ask yourself: "Does this align with my goals, or is it just going to make me regret later?" If the answer to that question is the latter, then you probably should give yourself permission to pass, whether that means skipping a party when your brain is begging for sleep or saying no to yet another responsibility when your to-do list already needs tending to.

Prioritization, though, isn't just about cutting stuff out; trade-offs are also an essential part . Sometimes, even the coolest opportunities need to take a back seat so you can focus on what matters most. Picture yourself in a cafeteria with an overloaded tray. You can't pile on pizza, salad, dessert, AND that suspicious-looking soup without risking a major disaster. Life's the same way. You have to pick and choose. Maybe skipping your hobby for a while frees up time to focus on a project that's a stepping stone for your dream career. These trade-offs might sting at first (goodbye, pizza!), but they ensure you're investing in what truly supports your long-term goals.

So, next time you're feeling overwhelmed, remember: you don't have to say yes to everything, and you definitely don't need to juggle more than you can handle. Prioritization is all about cutting the fluff, keeping it real, and making intentional choices that help you crush your goals, One SMART step at a time.

STOP WHAT YOU'RE DOING AND START PRIORITIZING

In the daily hustle of life, stress can detract you from reaching your goals. But prioritization offers a way to reduce stress levels while giving you clarity, direction, and the ability to stop spiraling into chaos. The connection is simple: when you have a clear plan, you're not drowning in indecision. Instead, you're moving confidently toward your goals, knocking off any impediments in your way that can be brought by stress.

Beyond catering to scenarios that bring you stress, another very important thing that prioritization does is to help you prune your to-do list to give you a clear line of action. Without a plan, it's easy to get stuck in what is called analysis paralysis, a stagnant state where you're confused about what to do in order to move you towards your foals - where suddenly, every decision feels like a life-or-death situation. When you identify what actually matters and focus on that, you calm the mental chaos, get more done, and feel more in control of your life.

This also impacts your happiness levels as you get higher on life, and less stressed. When you know what's worth your time, you can focus your energy where it counts, instead of trying to do everything at once and ending up with a burnt-out brain. When you finally get rid of the junk, everything fits, and finding what you need is a breeze. People who master the art of prioritization report higher job satisfaction, better control over their responsibilities, and a healthier work-life balance (9 Benefits of Time Management Success Stories for Employees, 2024).

And this isn't just theory—real-life stories prove it works. Take Sarah, for example: a college student drowning in coursework, part-time jobs, and a mountain of personal commitments. Sound familiar? Sarah decided enough was enough and prioritized academics, scheduling her study sessions and aligning her work shifts accordingly. This resulted in better grades, less stress and meltdowns. Stories like Sarah's hit close to home because they show us what's possible when you prioritize what's important to you.

To create a mental space where clarity and calmness reign supreme, and you can prioritize like a boss, you must take stock of factors around you that may prevent you from creating or having the enabling environment to prioritize. For instance, a messy desk or cluttered room can make your brain feel stuffy and clogged up. On the other hand, if you were to walk into a clean, organized space where everything is in its place, your brain will be instantly calm, creating a healthy mental space to perform this sorting act. Letting go of unnecessary worries or unimportant tasks will declutter your mind, and is twice as liberating.

To do this, you have to start small. Look around, and ask yourself, is your workspace giving off chaotic energy? If yes, fix it. Tidy up your desk, organize your digital files, or finally get rid of those five million unread emails. While at it, take a mental inventory. Write down all your stressors (yes, all of them!). Then, sort them out. What needs to be done right now ? What can wait? What can you hand off to someone else? This isn't about creating some structure that's set in stone. It's building a flexible system that keeps you focused while leaving room for curveballs that life may throw your way.

Ini doing this, you're not just relieving stress, you're setting the stage for a smoother, happier, and more productive life. Remember, prioritization isn't about doing it all; it's doing what needs must. So, go ahead, mind the business that pays you before all else.

WRAP UP

In this chapter, we've dived headfirst into the wonderful, slightly nerdy world of the Eisenhower Matrix and how it can morph the tornado that is your daily life into a light breeze. By figuring out the difference between what's urgent (hello, essay due tomorrow) and what's important (like sleeping and not turning into a stress zombie), you've unlocked a game-changing tool to sift through the noise. And no, this isn't just about giving your to-do list a glow-up. It's about reducing stress, boosting productivity, and finally balancing work, school, and your social life without feeling like you're juggling flaming swords.

Tossing distractions into the "Eliminate" quadrant feels like a small win—kind of like finding an extra fry at the bottom of your bag—but those little wins add up. Before you know it, you're not just busy; you're purposeful. And let's face it, that's the ultimate glow-up: going from "help, I'm drowning in tasks" to "look at me, thriving and taking names."

Here's the secret sauce: flexibility. Life is messy. One week you're cruising along, the next it's exam season, and suddenly you're planning a surprise birthday party for your bestie. The Eisenhower matrix is like your trusty sidekick, helping you focus on what matters right now while staying ready to pivot when life throws a curveball. It's not about being perfect—it's about being adaptable and staying sane.

Imagine not just surviving the chaos, but actually thriving because you know what really matters. Prioritization stops being a boring chore and turns into your secret weapon for a more enjoyable, less stressful life. Embrace it, tweak it, and let it lead the way. Your future self—chill, productive, and guilt-free—will be grateful.

PART III:
BUILDING MENTAL STRENGTH

CHAPTER 6:
DIGITAL DETOX: THE ART OF SHUTTING DOWN YOUR MENTAL OVERLOAD

Every now and again, it's important to close out all those open tabs you swore you'd get back to, but never did. You want a total refresh. Vert often, you need that much-needed breather from the constant buzz of notifications, endless scrolling, and the multi-platform chaos that's now somewhat engulfed your brain on a full-time basis. This chapter dives into how to help you achieve that. First, we uncover why we're so glued to our screens and how this non-stop digital connection is turning our brains into slow, glitchy browsers. Too many tabs open? Yeah, no wonder it's crashing.

Also, we dig into why social media, email overload, and those "innocent" late-night Netflix binges are secretly sabotaging your mental clarity; why our mind is now a computer struggling to function due to an overwhelming array of apps and to-do's – Think Instagram, TikTok, Spotify, and 15 half-read articles all open at once. It's no wonder you're feeling drained. The good bit is, just like our computer's browse, your brain functions a lot better once you start closing those tabs.

In this chapter, you'll learn how to tame the digital chaos and set boundaries without shutting off the world. We'll explore practical strategies to manage the constant connectivity that sneaks into every corner of your life, from cleaning out your inbox, avoiding social media black holes, to finally putting down your phone at 2 a.m. to give your brain some well-deserved rest.

By the end, you'll find out how to spot sneaky distractions that drain your energy and reclaim your focus to set you on the path to a more balanced, mindful relationship with technology; a relationship where you're in control and not the other way around. So, get ready to declutter your mental desktop and push the "off" switch on all that digital noise.

UNCOVERING THE SNEAKY TECH HABITS THAT DESTROY THE PEACE

Pretty much most of the time it starts this way: You're curled up on the couch, phone in hand, planning to "just check a couple of updates" on social media. Fast forward an hour, and you've spiraled through puppy videos, a celebrity's avocado toast tutorial, and a blown-out disagreement in the comments section about what randomers think of pineapple on pizza. Somehow, you've gone from "just a minute" to "where did my time go?" crisis. Well, if you didn't know this, social media is the ultimate rabbit hole; the silent thief of your focus. This is why it's important to manage your social media activity.

Another digital monster is your overflowing email inbox. Opening it feels like cracking open a closet stuffed to the brim—emails tumbling out like mismatched socks and expired coupons. Every unread message is screaming, "Read me! Respond NOW!" Meanwhile, you're mentally cluttered, and your inbox has turned into a chaos factory. Well, it's not all grim. A little organization can tame this beast—setting specific times to clear out the digital clutter and sort the "urgent" from the "unsubscribe" can do wonders for your sanity.

The seductive siren song of streaming services are just as much as a worthy culprit you must pay attention to as well. "Just one more episode," you say, settling in for a quick peek at a new series. Before you know it, it's 3 a.m., you've finished an entire season, and your responsibilities are judging you from the corner of the room. Binge-watching seems harmless until it starts hijacking your to-do list. Sure, unraveling a plot twist is fun, but not when it leaves you sleep-deprived and procrastinating on that project due since yesterday.

Speaking of hijacking, let's talk notifications. They tug at your attention, like a relentless toddler. Pinging, buzzing, and flashing every time you try to focus. Suppose you're reading a book, and someone keeps tapping you on the shoulder to tell you random trivia. This is what notifications do to your brain. They fragment your attention, crank up your stress, and leave you wondering why you opened your phone in the first place. Before you know it, you're trapped in a cycle of interruptions, irritability, and mental exhaustion.

All these digital distractions (including social media, email overload, binge-watching, and notifications) are not just a thief of your precious time. They hijack the mental clarity you need to be creative and focus. These tools, designed to keep us connected, can end up tethering us so tightly to our screens that we miss out on meaningful connections and creativity in real life.

Thankfully, recognizing the problem is half the battle conquered. When you start noticing how these habits take hold, you can begin to reclaim your time and mental space. Technology isn't the enemy; it's how we use it that matters. With a little awareness and some simple tweaks, you can strike a balance between enjoying the perks of the digital world and staying in control of your sanity.

Start small. Limit your screen time, and set aside time to declutter your inbox like you're spring-cleaning. Set a bedtime for your Netflix binges (and please, stick to it!), and mute your notifications when trying to focus. In making these intentional choices, you're not just regaining time, you're creating space for your brain to breathe, relax, and maybe even think up your next big idea. Achieving balance isn't about ditching the digital world; it's about controlling your use without letting it use you.

MASTERING THE ART OF TECH-FREE TIME

Successfully participating in the digital world without letting it completely hijack your life might seem a small victory. But it's largely important. Step one? Establish some tech-free times. Let's say you've had a long day, and instead of doom-scrolling until your thumb cramps, you carve out one glorious hour to do something screen-free. Maybe you crack open a book, experiment with a new recipe, or attempt a yoga pose that makes you look more like a human pretzel than a wellness guru. Whichever thing you do, you will find that the intentional break will work wonders for your brain and keep burnout at bay.

Now, let's talk about limiting daily screen time. This doesn't have to mean going cold turkey on your loved ones. It can be as little (yet significant) as a gentle nudge to stop staring at your phone and pursue real life connections. And there are apps for this, with UX built to be non-judgmental, so they may say something like "Hey, maybe it's time to step away from TikTok." These in-app nudges help you track your screen time, giving you an eye-opening look at just how much of your life is spent swiping. And really, taking small steps to reduce that time can lead to big changes in the world beyond your screen.

For those moments when your phone feels like a digital minefield of pings and dings (especially during work hours), the "Do Not Disturb" feature should be your knight in shining armor. Example. You're trying to focus on an assignment, and suddenly, your group chat explodes in a heated debate about the superior pizza topping. With your "Do Not Disturb" on, all those interruptions disappear, leaving you in a beautiful, notification-free bubble of productivity. This gives you the time and focus you need to get stuff done faster, make fewer mistakes, and actually earn guilt-free time to do other things.

Speaking of boundaries, let's talk about the people in your life. Setting tech boundaries with friends and family can save your sanity. Be honest about needing some offline time to prioritize your mental health. Most people will get it, and for those who don't, at least they might stop sending you memes at 2 a.m. Once they're on board, you might even inspire them to join you in a little digital detox. Who knows? Maybe it turns into a group effort, and suddenly, you're all reconnecting in ways that don't involve emojis.

The magic of those offline moments is that conversations flow uninterrupted, shared activities feel more meaningful, and silence becomes a welcome companion instead of something awkward to fill with GIFs. You'll then realize that deep, meaningful connections don't need a "like" button to thrive.

When you embrace these strategies, you'll start to see how constant connectivity was draining your mental battery. By stepping back and recalibrating, you give yourself the gift of clarity. You'll find the intentional social media break to be not only refreshing, but transformative. You'll have more energy, sharper focus, and some newfound appreciation for the world outside your screen. So go ahead, unplug a little. Your brain will thank you, and who knows? You might even discover that life offline isn't so bad after all.

MULTITASKING: WHEN DOING IT ALL MEANS DOING NOTHING WELL

In our tech-obsessed world, multitasking is often hyped as a superpower. Who wouldn't want to reply to emails, attend a Zoom meeting, and microwave lunch all at the same time? But here's the truth bomb: multitasking is less "superpower" and more "super flop." So it turns out, 'single-tasking' works better for productivity. But let's dive into why focusing on one thing at a time is the way to go, and explore some ways you can master this deceptively simple skill .

First off, science says multitasking is basically a scam. When you think you're doing multiple things at once, you're really just bouncing back and forth between tasks faster than a squirrel on caffeine. This constant switching doesn't just make you less efficient—it makes you more prone to mistakes (Batuhan Odabaş, 2024). We've all tried writing that all-important email while half-listening to a Zoom call, only to realize you addressed your boss as "Mom" rather than "Ma'am"? Yeah... Not your finest moment.

But the beauty of single tasking lies in the elevation of the simple. Studies have shown that when you give your undivided attention to one task, you're not just faster, you're also better at it (Why Multitasking Is a Myth and How to Truly Be Efficient, 2024). Think of the last time you worked on something without distractions. Just you, your task, and maybe a snack for moral support. Didn't it feel satisfying to finish without your brain oscillating between multiple commitments? That's the power of single tasking at work.

So why do we cling to the myth of multitasking? It's a romantic idea that feels productive. Switching between tasks gives the illusion of getting more done, but in reality, you're not accomplishing much. Eventually, something will crash; juggling multiple balls, you'll eventually fumble one (or two, or all). Multitasking overloads your brain, leaving you frazzled, exhausted, and wondering why your to-do list keeps getting longer (Batuhan Odabaş, 2024).

A technique that will help you blast through tasks with single-tasking is the Pomodoro Technique. Think of it as workout for your brain, minus the sweating. Here, you work on a task for 25 minutes, then take a five-minute break. Rinse and repeat. It's simple, effective, and gives your brain those micro-recharges it desperately needs. As a bonus, there's something deeply satisfying about telling yourself, "Just XYZ minutes," and realizing you actually got stuff done within that period – You earn yourself a good dopamine kick.

It goes without saying that single-tasking takes practice, and little discipline. You start by honestly singling out tasks that need your full attention (hint: probably not scrolling TikTok). Set boundaries, use timers, and politely inform your phone notifications that they're on mute for now. Over time, single-tasking will come more naturally.

Mindfulness is another secret weapon in your single-tasking arsenal. Mindfulness is simply about being present and focused. A quick deep-breathing exercise before you start a task or a short walk to clear your head can work wonders for your concentration and give your brain the required pep talk like, "Hey, we got this, let's just do this one thing and we advance to the next."

Combining these strategies will set you up for success. You'll make decisions faster, solve problems more efficiently, and still have enough brainpower left to conquer Wordle in record time. Single-tasking isn't just about getting stuff done; it's about doing it with intention and purpose. So go on and go all in. Lock in. But first, shut those extra tabs, and let it be one task at a time. Your mind (and quite likely, your boss) will thank you.

DITCH THE PRESSURE, KEEP YOUR PEACE

Today's world of endless screens and constant alerts means we all have to swim against the tides of distractions and attention thieves. These don't just mess with our schedules, they also clutter our mental space and make life feel slow. It's noisy, frustrating, and definitely not smooth sailing.

But once you see these patterns for what they are—time-stealing, brain-draining chaos—you've got the power to take back control., and carve out moments of focus and calm amidst the digital storm.

You may ask, what is the secret to breaking free? Boundaries. Glorious, life-changing boundaries. Intentional tech-free moments are like little vacations for your brain. Tools like screen-time apps and the magical "Do Not Disturb" feature can help you reclaim your day. They're like personal bouncers that keep distractions out the door of your productivity where you actually get stuff done.

Beyond you, boundaries must to be set for your loved ones, too (including friends and family). Let your loved ones know about your new tech habits so they can respect your downtime. When everyone's on the same page, it not only strengthens your focus, but also improves your relationships with these people.

The key here is small, intentional steps. Very little changes like setting aside 15 minutes for screen-free reading or turning off notifications during dinner can lead to big shifts in how you engage with technology. Instead of letting it run the show, you become the one calling the shots. And guess what? That balance is what you need to constantly thrive in a world that's always buzzing.

So unplug, take a breath, and rediscover the joy of living without constant distractions. It's not about ditching technology entirely (we still love memes and puppy videos); Find a healthier way to coexist. Your brain will thank you, your relationships will thank you, and you might fall in love with the journey to discovering or unlocking your purpose again.

CHAPTER 7: MINDFULNESS FOR THE REAL WORLD

Nothing quite captures the concept of having the presence of mind like mindful living. It's all about soaking up the present moment, and can be found in the little, seemingly mundane things. For instance, actually tasting your coffee instead of chugging it. Sure, it might sounds simple, but let's be real: with life throwing distractions our way, it can be tough to stay in the moment and be truly grateful. This is important because gratitude can be a surprisingly powerful (and totally free) tool to unlock a more mindful way of living.

When you start your day by appreciating the little things—a perfectly brewed cup of coffee, a text from a friend that makes you smile, or even that fleeting moment when the Wi-Fi works flawlessly— you take stock of things and moments in your life that you won't have otherwise paid attention to. Beyond fluffy, feel-good moments, these moments are game-changers for how you see the world.

In this chapter, we'll break down how to sprinkle gratitude into your everyday life without turning it into another to-do list item. First on this list of tips we'll be sharing is journaling. A quick note about something you're thankful for can flip your mindset from scarcity to abundance. You'll also learn how showing gratitude to others doesn't just make you a nicer human—it deepens relationships and might even get you more invites to brunch.

There is enough medical research to support the notion that gratitude comes bearing mental health benefits, too. From lowering stress to helping you sleep better. It's like your brain gets a little spa day every time you say, "Thank you." Pairing up a habit of Gratitude with mindfulness practices, will stack up the good vibes more than you ever thought it will.

When you're done with this chapter, you'll have a whole toolkit for turning ordinary days into gratitude-packed adventures. You'll know how to find joy in the small stuff and connect more deeply with others by simply saying "Thank you". So, grab a journal, take a breath, and get ready to turn your daily grind into a gratitude goldmine.

GRATITUDE IS THE POWER MOVE THAT SETS YOU FREE

It idea of intentional gratitude might strike you like something your grandma would sermonize about, but done right, it'll add more joy and positivity to your life. Rather than obsess over what's going wrong, start noticing the good stuff. It could be a sunny walk, a surprise text from a friend, or that perfectly brewed cup of coffee that finally hits just right.

Keeping a gratitude journal is where you take things to the next level with in a way that helps you stay conscious of the good happenings in your own life. It can be a reassuring resource for you to flip through these memories on tough days. A gratitude journal with make those small joys feel like lifelines. And there's no "right" or "wrong" way to do it. It doesn't matter if you're jotting down a single line or doodling hearts around the things you're thankful for. Once you have genuine appreciation, you're right on track. The science around this practice says it reduces anxiety and boosts happiness (Chowdhury, 2019). So, it's basically therapeutic, and that's way cheaper therapy that's more beneficial.

Unlike what most people think, gratitude is not a one-person thing. It's a team sport. Thanking others will further spread the positivity around. And when you take a moment to genuinely thank someone, be it for their support, their kindness, or just for existing, you strengthen your bonds with them and make their day better too.

Studies have now even shown that gratitude improves happiness and life satisfaction for both the giver and the receiver (Algoe, 2012). Beyond warming hearts, a heartfelt "thank you" will build bridges and create relationships that thrive on mutual encouragement and care.

Now, if you want to take your gratitude game to the next level, bring mindfulness along for the ride. Picture yourself sitting quietly, focusing on your breath, and acknowledging the things you're grateful for in that moment. Mindful gratitude is a way to help you sharpen your focus on being thankful for life, connecting the feeling to the present and making it feel more real. Those few minutes of quiet reflection can be the calm oasis on your chaotic days.

The science of gratitude is indeed fascinating. Gratitude isn't just good for your mood; it can improve sleep, boost physical health, and even reduce symptoms of anxiety and depression (Komase et al., 2021). Apparently, saying "thanks" will give your brain a good tune-up. Dr. Emmons even notes that gratitude can reduce inflammation and promote hope (Chowdhury, 2019). Who knew your mental and physical health could benefit from something as simple as appreciating your dog's goofy smile?

So, how can you best tap into a lifestyle of gratitude? Journaling. Set aside five minutes in the morning or before bed to write down three things you're grateful for. Get specific! Instead of "I'm grateful for food," try "I'm grateful for that pizza slice that had the perfect cheese pull." Make your journal fun—add stickers, doodles, or whatever makes it feel less like homework and more like a creative outlet.

And don't forget to thank the people around you. Start small: acknowledge kind gestures, and say "thanks" for everyday things, or write someone a quick note of appreciation. It's not about grand gestures. It's about consistent ones. Over time, you'll notice your relationships becoming warmer, like a cozy blanket of mutual respect and affection.

Finally, if mindfulness is your thing, combine it with gratitude. Take a few deep breaths, and reflect on one or two things that bring you joy. You don't need to meditate for hour. Just a few focused minutes can help you feel more present and grateful. Regular practice helps you spot more of life's little blessings, from the perfect sunset to the joy of finding money in an old jacket pocket.

And make no mistake: Gratitude isn't about pretending life's challenges don't exist. It's your way of finding balance and resilience amid these challenges. So, grab that journal, send that thank-you text, and take a mindful breath. You've got all the tools to turn your everyday life into a gratitude-filled adventure. And who knows? That next cup of coffee might taste even better with a kick of appreciation.

DO ONE THING WELL AND DITCH THE CIRCUS ACT

We live in a fast-paced world where multitasking can quickly feel like a badge of honor. I mean, who hasn't tried responding to an email, cooking pasta, and watching Netflix all at once? But you must know this: multitasking is not the productivity superpower people make it out to be. Focusing on one task at a time, what the pros call single-tasking, is where the real magic happens. So, let's unpack why doing one thing at a time is the optimal approach for your brain.

Productivity is a good place to start. When you multitask, your attention isn't split. It is, quite frankly, shattered . When you juggle multiple things means, you're barely skimming the surface of each task, like reading only the chapter titles of a book and pretending you've got the plot. Studies show that single-tasking lets you dive deep, engage fully, and actually finish stuff faster (Nevin, 2024). This means you're not just getting through tasks. You're actually immersing yourself enough in them to execute with precision. In this way, you're able to hit that flow state where everything just... clicks .

Your brain makes little negative reactions every time you switch tasks. It needs time to refocus, which eats up precious energy. It's been reported that multitasking can reduce your productivity by up to 40% (https://www.facebook.com/verywell , 2021). And in the fast-paced world we live in, it's the race equivalent of running a marathon with a broken shoelace.

When this happens, you're working harder, not smarter. On the other hand, doing one thing at a time keeps your brain humming like a well-oiled machine. No stalling, no mistakes, just pure efficiency.

Cognitive overload is when you have many things on your mind, and is a by-product of multi-tasking. If you've ever looked for your glasses while it was in your hand the whole time, year, you may be suffering from cognitive overload. The thing is, our brains aren't built to juggle a million things at once, and trying to do so just clutters your mental space. Single-tasking clears out that much of that space, giving your brain room to breathe and focus. So, rather than a chaotic tornado of thoughts, you get a calm, organized flow.

Besides just frying your focus, multitasking also increases your stress levels. Jumping between unfinished tasks can feel like running on a treadmill that never slows down. Whereas, single-tasking does the exact opposite: it's like walking off that treadmill, taking a deep breath, and saying, "One thing at a time." When you complete a task before moving on to the next, you'll get a sweet sense of accomplishment and calm. The high you get from cross crossing something off your to-do list is right up there with the most ecstatic of feelings.

Ever seen a baker decorating a cake or an artist lost in their work? That's single-tasking at work right there. Even the most mundane chores can get you into flow state. From washing dishes, to organizing your closet, or even writing an essay, everything becomes oddly satisfying when you're fully present and in the moment without letting your mind wander. So, rather than rush over tasks to check boxes off your to-do list, you're experiencing the task, noticing the details, and maybe even finding some creativity and joy along the way.

Ready to start single-tasking? Good. Begin by prioritizing your to-do list. Rank tasks based on urgency and importance, then tackle them one at a time. Create "focus zones" (these are blocks of uninterrupted time where you commit to one task and ignore everything else (and yes, that includes TikTok scrolling). Let your friends and coworkers know you're in the zone, so they don't hit you up with "urgent" texts that end up being not-so-urgent.

You also want to set clear goals for each session. Feeling fancy? Try the pomodoro technique, where you work for 25 minutes, then take a 5-minute break. Its giving your brain a treat after a 'solid workout'. Plus, it keeps you from burning out while still smashing your goals.

Now, make no mistake. Single-tasking isn't just about efficiency. It's about being present. Savor the little victories, like finishing a project or realizing your mind feels clearer when you're not juggling a million things. Even routine tasks can feel meaningful when you're fully engaged. You might even discover hidden perks like how organizing your sock drawer is weirdly therapeutic.

But that is not say you should be incapable of multitasking. Some multitasking is fine. Listening to a podcast while folding laundry? Why not?. But when it comes to tasks that need brainpower, like studying or writing an important email, you should single-task yourself till completion. Your brain will thank you, your stress levels will drop, and you'll finally get that sweet sense of accomplishment when the task is over and you aced it.

So, next time you're tempted to multitask, remember: single-tasking isn't boring. It's your secret weapon for slaying your to-do list and keeping your sanity intact. And hey, if it also means fewer typos in your emails, that's a win for everyone.

MAKING MINDFULNESS A DAILY HABIT

Very often, young adults and college students tend to get embroiled in a never-ending struggle that involves academic deadlines on the one hand, and personal life drama in the other. Somewhere in between, an attempt to eat, sleep, and function like a human also takes center-stage. When this happens, life then becomes a chaotic circus act. This is where the art of mindful living can help you strike a fine balance. In sprinkling a little dose of mindfulness into your daily routine, you can turn that overwhelming chaos for a sense of calm and clarity. Much like hitting the "shuffle" button on your mental playlist and finding the perfect song.

One effective way to kick off this mindfulness journey is by creating morning rituals. Rather than wake up to your alarm and immediately enter into panic mode over what to wear, or the little things, like whether you have milk for cereal, you ease into your day like a pro. Setting up and keeping to a morning ritual will not only set the tone for the day but also eliminates the dreaded "decision fatigue," which is the ultimate time waste. Decision fatigue is a real issue that crops up when your brain gets so tired from deciding stuff that is straightforward and makes it feel so impossible. Here's how to fix it: Start your morning with deep breathing, a short meditation, or even a slow stretch session (Staff, 2023). Try to do things to make your life easier, like pre-deciding simple stuff the night before (e.g., your outfit or breakfast). In this way, you save your mental energy for the big things. (Staff, 2023).

As the day unfolds, you must seize every opportunity to tap into the power of mindfulness. Don't just save it for the big moments. Eating lunch? Skip the multitasking and actually enjoy your food's taste. It might sound pretty straightforward, but seriously, when's the last time you noticed how amazing your sandwich was instead of scrolling. Those boring walks to class or work are also secretly golden opportunities for mindful exploration. Tune into the sounds around you, admire the trees, or notice how many people are also staring at their phones while walking. Suddenly, life feels a little more alive and a lot less robotic (tepliczky.peter, 2024).

The best evenings are spent winding down. Rather than collapse into bed with your brain still buzzing like a phone on silent, consider setting up a chill wind-down routine. This could mean reading a book (not a textbook), taking a warm bath (cue candles for ultimate spa vibes), or doing some gentle yoga stretches (bonus points if you don't fall asleep mid-pose) (Staff, 2023). These small rituals signal to your body and brain that it's time to power down. Plus, quality sleep is basically a cheat code for handling stress like a pro (tepliczky.peter, 2024).

Routines are not a one-size-fits-all, nor should they be. Life can be unpredictable. One day you're breezing through your schedule, and the next, you're fending off three last-minute deadlines and a group chat explosion. The gist is, flexibility is one effective way to keep your mindfulness juices flowing. Your routine should be personal to you – a playlist you can rejig and shuffle at any time, not some setlist carved in stone. When you adjust to what you need to do today, rather than stress about tomorrow, these habits stick. In this way, you'll stay engaged, balanced, and ready to tackle whatever curveballs life throws your way, with a touch calmer and a lot less chaos.

MINDFULNESS IS PEACE BY DESIGN: BUILDING A LIFE THAT ACTUALLY FEELS GOOD

Living life in the moment places us in a rare, refreshing place where suddenly everything feels a little more connected. Gratitude is the secret sauce that helps us tap into this elusive state. Whether it's jotting down what you're thankful for in a journal or giving someone a heartfelt "thanks", these small acts can sprinkle a little joy on the most chaotic days. It helps us to hit the pause button on life, so we can vibe in the moment, and realize it's not so bad after all.

With gratitude, your life can turn from a never-ending sprint to a leisurely stroll with scenic pit stops. When we shift our focus to what's good right now, whether that killer sunset, a perfectly made cup of coffee, or a dog that made eye contact and totally understood your soul, our life starts to feel less like a race against time and more like a journey worth savoring. In any case, practicing gratitude requires that we ground ourselves in the here and now. In this way, we can appreciate the beauty of today without getting lost in the drama of yesterday or the stress of tomorrow.

As we've explored in this chapter, practicing gratitude doesn't require grand gestures or complicated rituals. Just keep it simple and genuine. You'd be surprised how far little acknowledgments can go in reminding us that the present is worth noticing. Gratitude brings us closer to the people, experiences, and moments that make life richer. A refreshing change from multitasking your way through the day or worrying about things beyond your control is when you pause to acknowledge that you're here, enjoying the now.

CHAPTER 8:
HOW SMALL CHANGES IN YOUR MIND LEAD TO BIG WINS

In many ways, building healthy habits can be likened to assembling IKEA furniture: it requires a ton of effort, a bit of patience, and maybe a few moments where you question your decision to build these habit. Eventually, it ends up being worth it. Each small, consistent step builds a bridge to mental wellness, piece by piece. And it doesn't matter whether it's starting your morning with a stretch or sneaking in a few deep breaths during a chaotic study break. These little moves stack up, and over time, they create a path to feeling more in control and less like life is a tornado you're just trying to survive. Your mind is a garden. Plant a few good habits, water them with some consistency, and your mental health is sure to bloom.

In this chapter, we're diving into the surprisingly fun (and sometimes awkward) process of building routines that support mental health. Let this be your cheat sheet to a clearer, more balanced life. Exercise, for instance, is like a free ticket to happiness. It boosts your mood, sharpens your brain, and doesn't require a prescription. Your food is also worth considering for obvious reasons – You are what you eat. Plus, your food has a way of influencing how you feel. Then there's sleep, the underrated MVP of mental wellness. A good night's rest isn't just for beauty, it's a body hack that can bring you the increased focus, less stress, and more clarity with which you can plan and execute on your days.

By the end of this chapter, you'll have a toolkit of practical, relatable ways to incorporate these elements into your life without feeling like you're changing too much in your life. Because fostering long-term mental wellness isn't about grand gestures. It's the small, manageable tweaks in detail that, over time, make a big difference. Let's get to it!

YOUR BRAIN LOVES A GOOD WORKOUT

Whenever life feel you're stuck in survival mode, remember that moving your body can do wonders for your mind. Breaking a sweat isn't just about helping you fit into your favorite jeans, it's hitting the refresh button for your brain.

First, let's chat about the MVPs of mental wellness: endorphins. These little mood-boosting chemicals are basically your brain's way of saying, "Hey, you're doing great!" Exercise gets them flowing, and suddenly, you're feeling like a happier, less-stressed version of yourself. It's like your brain just booked itself a mini spa day (but without the cucumber slices!). Sure, your muscles may remind you that they exist, but it's worth it for that triumphant feeling. The science backs this up, too. According to The Science Behind Exercise and Mental Well-Being, regular physical activity can significantly reduce anxiety and provide a natural escape from stress (kingry, 2024).

Besides your mood, your brain also benefits. Exercise is like brain food, but rather than kale, it's movement. Regular activity boosts neuroplasticity - a fancy way of saying your brain gets better at learning, remembering, and solving problems. You've probably noticed how ideas just click after a quick walk. That's no coincidence. Moving your body stimulates new neural connections, making you sharper and more focused. According to research, when you're stuck on a problem, stepping away to stretch or jog can trigger those "aha!" moments (Exercise and Mental Health: 8 Benefits for Your Mood, 2024). So next time you're staring blankly at your to-do list, consider doing something cardio-friendly. It might just unlock your inner genius.

The best bit? You don't have to go it alone. Group exercise pulls double duty – both as a workout for your body and a boost for your social life. Whether it's a yoga class, a jogging club, or a dance crew where no one judges your awkward moves, being active with others adds a new layer of benefits. You'll build social bonds, share a few laughs, and maybe even grab a celebratory smoothie afterward. As a bonus, working out with friends creates accountability. Because, let's be real, it's harder to skip leg day when your buddy's waiting for you at the gym. These group experiences provide a sense of belonging, and we all know how feelings of connection is just as good for the soul as it is for the abs.

So, if you're hitting the gym, dancing in your living room, or jogging with your crew, take a step. Every move you make will nudge you towards a clearer mind and a brighter mood. Think of it this way: if you're smiling and sweating, you're doing it right.

FEEDING YOUR BRAIN THE GOOD STUFF, NOT THE JUNK

What you eat affects your brain. Think of your brain as the engine of a race car, revving 24/7, fueling your thoughts, memories, and the odd late-night ideas. But what happens if you pour soda into the tank? Yeah, not ideal. The thing is, your brain needs premium-grade fuel, and that's where nutrition comes in.

And let's not get it wrong, eating nutrient-rich foods isn't just about being fancy; it's about stabilizing your mood, boosting cognitive performance, and giving your brain the VIP treatment it deserves.

Nutrients like fruits, veggies, whole grains, and lean proteins are like a dream team of vitamins, minerals, and antioxidants (Selhub, 2022). Antioxidants, in particular, are like your brain's shield from oxidative stress, basically the brain's equivalent of an engine rust. So, every time you chow down on some blueberries or spinach, you're basically arming your neurons with tiny superhero shields. Sounds fancy?

Meanwhile, a humble glass of water is not to be overlooked as it has its role to play. Staying hydrated keeps your brain from staging a protest. Ever felt cranky or sluggish for no apparent reason? That's dehydration. Drinking some water can help transport nutrients, flush out waste, and sustain brain function. In this way, it works like the oil an engine (your brain) needs to prevent friction. So when next you're feeling snappy, maybe chug a glass of H2O before blaming your bad mood on the group chat drama.

Sugary snacks and processed foods can be tempting. Let's be real: who doesn't want a donut or a candy bar after a long day? The problem is, they carry a short-lived energy high, which is usually followed by a dreaded crash; A real roller coaster ride for your brain, that leaves you with brain fog and a bland mood (Selhub, 2022). As such, cutting back on these foods can be a game-changer for your mental clarity and emotional balance.

Your gut and brain are connected. Your gut microbiome, a term for the bacteria living in your belly, produces serotonin, the "feel-good" neurotransmitter that helps regulate your mood. So, when you're feeding your gut healthy stuff like fiber and plant-based foods, you're essentially feeding your gut with a healthy dose of serotonin (Selhub, 2022), and you know what they say - a happy gut equals a happy brain. Who knew eating a salad could be so emotionally fulfilling?

Omega-3 fatty acids are also worth considering. Found in fish, flaxseeds, and walnuts, these fatty acids are proven mood boosters and cognitive enhancers (Gómez-Pinilla, 2008). Prepping meals with these ingredients not only saves you from the temptation of fast food but also gives your brain the TLC it deserves.

Much has been said about the benefits of hydration. But all knowledge is useless if not implemented. So to incorporate hydration in your life, set reminders, carry a trendy water bottle, or challenge yourself to chug a glass every time you check your phone. And for those snack attacks, swap sugary treats for whole foods like nuts or fruit. Do this and your future self will thank you. These small, manageable tweaks will, over time, turn into powerful habits that help you treat your brain like the star it is.

RECHARGE YOUR MIND BY SLEEPING YOUR WAY TO CALM

The unsung hero of mental wellness, quality sleep is like the friend who quietly holds your life together while you go through a mid-life crisis. Yet, for too many young adults, prioritizing sleep can be difficult. But here's the kicker: If you treat sleep right, it'll treat you right back with better mental health, sharper thinking, and fewer sloppy moments.

Let's start with the brain. While you're snoozing, your brain isn't just chilling; it's basically Marie Kondo-ing your memories. It's sorting through all the day's information, deciding what's worth keeping (like the answer to question 12 on your quiz) and what's not (like your classmate's lunch rant). Skipping sleep, though? That can be like closing a laptop without saving your work. The research hints that sufficient sleep consolidates memories and boosts your ability to learn new things, making it critical for productivity (Suni & Dimitriu, 2024).

If sleep deprivation can be this costly, then what's it impact on your emotions? When you don't get enough sleep, your brain is unable to regulate emotions. Suddenly, every small inconvenience feels like the end of the world. Studies link poor sleep patterns to increased anxiety and depressive symptoms, turning you into a walking bundle of stress (Desai et al., 2024).

Enter your body's internal clock, (also known as your circadian rhythm). This concept dictates when you feel awake and when you fall asleep. Syncing this rhythm by going to bed and waking up at the same time every day, even on weekends, helps train your body to fall asleep faster and sleep better. It's like teaching your brain to be a reliable alarm clock. (Desai et al., 2024).

Without sleep, your decision-making will be messy. Problem-solving? Glitchy. That big exam or job interview? Yikes. Lack of sleep doesn't just slow you down; it flat-out hijacks your cognitive abilities (Suni & Dimitriu, 2024). Ever tried making sense of a group project after an all-nighter? Exactly.

Then there's the magic of REM sleep. This is where your brain gets extra fancy, processing complex emotions and solidifying memories. It's like your personal emotional therapist, sorting through the chaos of your day without judgment. For college student navigating everything from exam stress to messy roommate drama, REM sleep is basically free therapy you can't afford to skip (Desai et al., 2024).

But how do you make sleep a priority in a world where a lot is fighting for your attention? Start by engineering your environment to enable sleep. Invest in comfy bedding, hang some blackout curtains, and consider a white noise machine if you have noisy neighbors. Then, establish a wind-down routine an hour before bed. You could swap your phone for a book, do some light stretching, or take a warm bath. Your brain will take the hint that it's time to power down (Suni & Dimitriu, 2024).

There are also some don'ts to follow. Chugging caffeine at 9 PM or demolishing a double cheeseburger right before bed is a No-no. These habits mess with your sleep cycles, and while a glass of wine might feel relaxing, alcohol disrupts your REM sleep. So save those lattes and late-night munchies for earlier in the day.

All in all, consistency is key. Your body loves a good routine, and sticking to a regular sleep schedule will pay off big time. In making these small, manageable changes, you're not just investing in better sleep; you're building a foundation for mental wellness, better focus, and optimal brain function. Sleep tight. You've earned it, after all.

YOUR DAILY DOSE OF WELLNESS

We've explored in this chapter how building habits that support mental health can offer the stability we need as we navigate life's ups and downs. Exercise isn't just about getting those abs, it's your body's natural pick-me-up and chance to boost your mood with a splash of those feel-good endorphins. Your workout routine is both a solo adventure for mental clarity and an opportunity to socialize when you join others. These habits not only help clear your mind but also weave a community around shared goals, making the journey toward mental wellness a little less lonely.

From what we munch on to how we catch those precious Z's, every little habit counts. Nutrition plays the role of a trusty sidekick, offering the nourishment your brain craves while steering clear of those sugar-induced slumps. Then there's sleep, the unsung hero of mental well-being, which we need to keep stress at bay and emotions in check. Embracing these everyday habits will stack the odds ridiculously in favor of your stronger mental health. So why not give it a spin?

PART IV:
RESILIENCE AND JOY

CHAPTER 9:
WHEN LIFE BURNS, BRING SOME BANTER!

Laughter therapy is your brain's fun little way of hitting the "refresh" button. For instance, when you're drowning in deadlines, buried under exams, or spiraling about life in general, laughing probably feels like the last thing on your mind.

Think of it: That moment you're sharing a spontaneous laugh with friends, maybe over a meme so dumb it's genius, do you ever remember your worries? No. The thing is, laughter doesn't magically solve your problems, but it makes them feel a whole lot less intimidating. This is the essence of mental decluttering. Facing life's challenges with less tension rather than dodging them.

In this chapter, we'll geek out over the science of why laughter reduces stress, explore how it rewires your mood, and talk about the incredible ways it helps your body chill out. Even better, you'll learn practical tips for sneaking more humor into your daily routine.

When things go awry, humor can be the glue that holds your sanity together. We'll also show you how laughter builds stronger connections with the people you love and helps keep your mental clarity on point.

By the end, you'll see why laughter shouldn't feature as just a side dish in the buffet of life. It should be the main course for resilience, well-being, and actually enjoying the ride.

FROM PANIC ATTACKS TO LAUGH ATTACKS: HOW HUMOR MELTS STRESS

Laughter is the best medicine, or so they say. Unlike actual meds, laughter doesn't come with side effects. Rather, it comes with perks like instant mood boosts, social bonding, and the ability to momentarily forget stressors in your life.

Laughing makes your body kick into overdrive in the best way. It triggers the flow of endorphins, your body's 'feel-good' hormones. These little wonders flood your system, making you feel all warm and fuzzy while simultaneously kicking stress hormones like cortisol to the curb. And that's a big deal, because chronic stress and high cortisol levels are like those annoying pop-ups on your computer —they just won't let you live. (Why Laughter Is the Best Medicine for Your Whole Health, 2024)

In addition, laughter can also increases your ability to withstand pain. When you've stubbed your toe or are navigating some emotional drama, laughter reminds you that pain, be it physical or emotional, isn't the end of the world. It's your brain's little way of saying, "Chill, we've got this."

Another cool effect of laughing is in changing your perception of things. When life's pressure kicks in, all you need is a good laugh for that deadline to seem less terrifying, and personal issue to feel a bit less like a soap opera. In those times when you are spiraling, laughter will make the weight of the world lifted, even if only temporarily.

And let's not forget: laughter loves company. Sharing a laugh with friends is basically the social glue of human connection. You know, those moments when someone tells a ridiculous story, and everyone's laughing so hard they're crying? That shared hilarity doesn't just make for a good time. It strengthens relationships. It's why teammates bond over inside jokes or why you feel closer to someone after swapping memes for hours.

The science backs this up: people who laugh together form stronger connections and build trust faster. So basically, you can think of laughter as like a cheat code for friendship (10+ Scientifically Proven Ways Laughter Can Relieve Stress, 2019).

In professional or creative settings, a good laugh can break the tension and get ideas flowing. When people feel relaxed and free to toss out wacky ideas, innovation thrives. So yes, that silly pun your coworker made in the brainstorming meeting? It might've paved the way for the next big thing! In workplaces that embrace humor, employees are not only more engaged but also more likely to think outside the box. Laughter creates an environment where no idea is too "out there," which is exactly where groundbreaking ideas are born.

So, how do you bring more laughter into your life? Start small. Send a funny meme to your group chat, watch a comedy special, or try that silly Snapchat filter that makes everyone look like a talking potato. It's not about forcing yourself to laugh at everything (please don't become that person), but about inviting humor into your everyday routine.

When life throws you curveballs, let laughter be your personal shield. It'll not only make the tough moments bearable; it builds resilience, strengthens relationships, and sparks creativity. So the next time you're feeling overwhelmed, remember, the solution might just be simpler than you think. All you need is a good laugh and maybe a terrible dad joke. After all, life's too short to take it too seriously. Laugh it up, enjoy the ride! The Neuroscience of LOLs:

THE NEUROSCIENCE OF LOLS: COMEDY AS COGNITIVE NUTRITION

When you laugh, your brain goes all out to light up the pleasure centers and releases dopamine. Dopamine, the Queen Bee of body chemicals, lifts your mood, sharpens your decision-making skills, and makes figuring out life's quizzing puzzles a little easier..

But beyond its feel-good functions, it can help you cope better with stress. Imagine you're super-stressed over an exam, and your friend casually drops a light-hearted remark about how exams are overrated. Suddenly, the world feels less grim. You see, humor has this magical ability to reframe anxiety and stress, making even the biggest disasters feel manageable (or at least chuckle-worthy). It's like your brain's very own "delete" button that helps you reboot and tackle the problem with fresh eyes.

As a result, not only your brain benefits. Your body gets in on the action too. Laughing is basically cardio in disguise (and yes, we're claiming it's as beneficial as any other body workout). It gets your heart pumping, fills your lungs with oxygen, and even gives your immune system a little boost, thanks to those stress-fighting neuropeptides. It's like a spin class for your insides. No Lycra required. Moreover, it helps lower cortisol levels (Cortisol is the stress hormone ruining your sleep, and stopping you from dozing off like you would in a relaxed, calm state. So, if you're looking to ride on laughter's plentiful benefits for your body, maybe you're better off swapping the late-night doom-scrolling for a comedy special. Science claims it works wonders, after all. (Mayo Clinic Staff, 2023)

Serious laughter can come in healthy packages, too. An example of this is called Laughter therapy. Laughter therapy is fast becoming a go-to tool for mental health pros, especially due to its ability to cure conditions like depression and anxiety. It's basically therapy, but rather than cry into a tissue or clear your chest in front of a psychotherapist sat in front of you, you're basically cracking over jokes. These structured laughter sessions are designed to get people giggling in a safe, judgment-free zone, where stress hormones drop and endorphins increase. Think of it as your emotional CrossFit, where you give your emotions a good, healthy workout that sets you up for future stability. (Yim, 2016)

But what makes laughter therapy even cooler? It's a team sport. Laughing with others creates instant connections, even if you're bonding over the world's worst pun or a hilariously bad movie. Shared laughter builds community, strengthens relationships, and makes everyone feel a little less alone. It's like a universal language everyone understands, and benefits from. The best part? It can come in any way, shape, or form. Swapping dad jokes with coworkers? Laughing till your face hurts with friends? It doesn't matter. Those moments of shared hilarity make life's chaos feel a little less chaotic.

Little wonder humor is making its way into mainstream mental health practices. It's free, effective, accessible, and doesn't require a prescription (but that's not denying that a Netflix subscription might help). Whether you're in a formal laughter therapy session or just losing it over TikToks, finding ways to laugh can seriously improve your mental well-being. So, the next time life feels overwhelming, remember: the best cure might be a bad pun, a cat video, or a joke so cringe-worthy it loops back around to being funny. Sometimes, the simplest solution is just to laugh it off. One giggle at a time.

TURNING YOUR TO-DO LIST INTO A LOL LIST

When life's demands feel like they're closing in, humor can swoop in to save the day. There are times when powering through your do-do list can feel like the impossible jobs. And it can come in different forms. Let's say you're stuck in a soul-sucking meeting or crawling through traffic. Rather than simmer in frustration, your eyes suddenly wanders to your coworker's quirky pen-clicking habit or a bumper sticker that says, "Honk if you love tacos." And there you have it – an instant mood shift. You see, humor doesn't magically make the situation better, but in a world where things can quickly get hazy, hampering you from making smooth progress, humor can feel help in swapping out a blurry lens for one that shows life in 4K with bonus bloopers.

A humor-friendly environment is like a personal amusement park for your brain. Surround yourself with things that make you laugh, be it comedy posters, sticky notes with your favorite dumb jokes, or even that one absurd meme you can't stop chuckling over. Fill your breaks with comedy specials, stand-up routines, or TikToks so funny they make you snort-laugh. By curating a space that's a constant source of giggles, you're setting yourself up for easy access to joy (More, 2024). It'll be like planting laughter seeds and harvesting smiles all day long.

If you thought laughter is just for your own consumption, then you may be missing out on the bigger picture. Laughter is a social glue that turns acquaintances into squad goals. Playfully interact with the people around you, whether it's family, friends, or coworkers. Host board game nights that make you cry-laugh (Cards Against Humanity, anyone?), share cringe-worthy stories from your day, or stage impromptu karaoke battles. These goofy moments create stronger bonds and make even the dullest interactions feel like mini-parties. Sharing laughs will not only strengthens relationships but also lowers stress levels and tensions.

But to enjoy all of these benefits, you must stay open to humor, even on tough days. Life is full of absurdity if you know where to look. Maybe your pet pulls an epic fail trying to jump onto the couch, or a coworker accidentally makes a pun so bad it's good. These little gems are tiny reminders not to take life so seriously. Humor doesn't have to be forced; just let it bubble up naturally when the moment's right, and even the messiest days will feel a bit lighter.

Making humor a habit doesn't have to be complicated. Start with ten minutes of a comedy podcast during your commute or a quick meme scroll while waiting for your coffee. Identify the things that make you laugh—whether it's sarcastic one-liners, slapstick humor, or cat videos. Think of comedy as a playlist: what cracks one person up might make someone else groan. So, by all means, find and curate your "greatest hits" (Haupt, 2023).

Here's one way you can excel at this: Find one funny thing every day. It could be an overheard conversation on the subway, or maybe it's laughing at yourself for spilling coffee again. Training your brain to find humor in the little things of life will build your appetite for comedy, so you'll get better at spotting the funny stuff everywhere you go.

Humor isn't always spontaneous. It can be a skill you build. Join an improv class, go to a comedy club, or even try writing your own jokes. You'll gain a new appreciation for the mechanics of humor while surrounding yourself with people who value laughter just as much as you do. Plus, crafting your own jokes means not only are you laughing, you're now you're making others laugh, too, which increases your value to these people.

One word of caution, though. Your humor should never be at someone else's expense. A well-placed joke is like a warm hug; a mean-spirited one is like a slap in the face. Practice emotional intelligence when cracking jokes and ensure everyone feels included in the laughter. A good sense of humor uplifts and connects, creating a safe space where everyone can join in the fun without feeling left out (More, 2024).

Ultimately, the funniest moments are often the ones you don't see coming. Your friend's kid telling a nonsensical joke that somehow lands, or an unexpected sitcom twist that has you laughing until you cry. These unplanned bursts of hilarity are life's way of reminding you that joy is everywhere if you're open to it. So, let yourself get swept up in the ridiculousness of life. After all, a good laugh might not solve all your problems, but it sure makes them easier .

LIFE'S A JOKE, SO LAUGH IT OFF

Wrapping up this chapter about why laughs are the best thing for your mental clarity since sliced bread, one thing you should take away is that humor is basically your brain's secret weapon against stress. This means it's more than just a mere distraction, as you may have likely perceived it before. We' have explored how a good laugh can do everything from lowering stress levels to boosting your mood and even shifting your perspective when life feels like a bad reality show. Laughter takes those tense, "I can't even" moments and turns them into "Okay, maybe I can" moments. This mental hack offers you a much-needed breather and helping you tackle challenges without the emotional baggage.

In all of these, remember, humor is your get-out-of-jail-free card for stressing situations. It doesn't make problems magically disappear, but it does make them seem a whole lot less terrifying. That perspective shift is pure gold because it builds resilience, clears your head, and might even help you come up with actual solutions instead of imploding.

A bonus perk of adding laughs to your daily routine is that it helps you thrive, not just survive. Sharing a belly laugh with friends does more than just make you feel good in the moment. It strengthens your relationships, turning acquaintances into ride-or-die allies. And in creative spaces? Humor is the spark that gets the good ideas flowing. It breaks down barriers, encourages fresh thinking, and transforms a boring brainstorm into a comedy hangout - one where innovation reigns supreme.

As a college student trying to juggle exams, social life, and sleep, or a young adult navigating the wild world of adulting, you can lean on the power of humor as your mental reset button every now and again. Embrace the funny memes, the ridiculous puns, and the spontaneous giggle fits. Beyond the entertainment value on offer, you get a rewarding package of self-care disguised as silliness. So what's stopping you from laugh your way through the chaos? Do it. Your brain, your mood, and even your relationships will thank you for it!

CHAPTER 10: SMASH THAT RESET BUTTON AND GIGGLE YOUR WAY FORWARD

Finding humor in life's chaos helps us reset our minds, giving our brain a much-needed refresh or rejuvenation. it's washing away the sticky stress residue while making room for moments of joy and clarity. Life, as we know it, can be a master of mess-making. And it's not just your desk that's a disaster; your mind is probably holding onto every to-do list, random song lyric, and awkward memory it can ever recollect. But clearing out those cobwebs doesn't just help manage stress. It gives you a front-row seat to some of the funniest, most fulfilling parts of your life.

In this chapter, we'll roll out mental decluttering strategies that leverage comedic flair. These methods are the quirky cast of your personal sitcom, each playing a role in your quest for mental clarity. Task prioritization is the overachieving friend who loves a good list, while mindfulness practices are the chill surfer reminding you to breathe between laughs. Journaling is the reliable diary-keeper who loves tea and introspection, and boundary-setting is the bouncer at your brain's velvet rope, keeping the drama out. Self-care rituals? Well, think of them as the diva demanding that you control your narrative.

Life's script is unpredictable and full of plot twists that even the best writers couldn't dream up. But with these strategies, you'll stay light on your feet, rolling with the punches with humor as your co-pilot. As you find a laugh in your worst moments, you'll discover that mental clarity and humor go hand in hand. So grab the spotlight, embrace the absurd, and let your brain become the place where laughter and life coexist beautifully.

YOUR STRATEGY PLAYBOOK FOR QUICK WINS IN EVERYDAY LIFE

Before we conclude this epic adventure into the wild world of mental decluttering, let's revisit the strategies we've tackled—but this time, with a twist of comedy. Humor isn't just a mood-booster; it offers a way to remember things better when they're tied to a laugh (Henderson, 2015).

Prioritizing is first up. Your tasks are basically characters in a sitcom. Some are the charming lead actors demanding the spotlight, while others are the random coffee shop extras who can wait their turn. Give your attention to the stars of the show first. In other words, the tasks that need you now. The others can wait.

Mindfulness can useful given that your thoughts can be a conveyor belt of funny thoughts. Here, your job is to decide which one is worth keeping for the stand-up routine of life and which ones are just bad open-mic material. Letting the thoughts flow without grabbing onto the ones that don't bring joy is a brain decluttering hack.

There's also journaling. A blank page, a stage, and an audience of one (you!) is all you will ever need. Spill your thoughts about everything. Rant about the annoying Wi-Fi, or write that Oscar-worthy screenplay about your dog's secret life. It doesn't matter whether these entries are deep or meant to be just hilariously random thoughts – the impact of the journaling process is to help you turn the turn mental chaos you're feeling in the present into something worth applauding (or at least re-reading for a laugh).

You also need to set boundaries. if you were a bouncer at a comedy club, not every act will get to go on stage. In the same way, not every thought or task will deserve your attention. Learn to say "no" with the confidence of a mic-dropping comedian. Save your energy for the acts that deserve a standing ovation, not the ones destined for awkward silence.

Self-care? Oh, that's one of life's necessity. It doesn't matter if you're merely binging your favorite sitcom, indulging in ice cream for dinner, or singing in the shower like no one's listening, self-care is your intermission. It's the reset button that keeps you sane between life's plot twists.

Since you would make progress along your journey, you need to visualize your roadmap. Imagine you're holding a scrapbook filled with funny snapshots, goofy milestones, and maybe even a glittery timeline of your achievements. When you see how far you've come, you're motivated to stay the course. It's a bit like watching bloopers from your favorite show. It reminds us that growth is nothing but a series of imperfect, hilarious moments where you figure things out as you progress.

These strategies are easy to integrate into your life. Revisit them whenever life starts feeling like a drama, and they'll remind you that laughter is the best mental organization tool.

As we mentioned in previous chapters, laughter is rooted in science. It doesn't only make you feel good; it rejuvenates your brain, making it easier to retain information and stay motivated (Moeinian, 2024). So, as you implement these strategies, do it with a smile (or a full-on belly laugh). Your brain, and your stress levels, will thank you.

Ultimately, you may think of these strategies (the art of prioritizing, mindfulness, journaling, boundary-setting, self-care, and visualization) as your 'mental wellness avengers'. With humor as your co-pilot, keeping your mind clear and stress-free becomes less of a chore and more of an enjoyable ride.

THE MIND WORKOUT FOR A LIFETIME OF CALM

Mental decluttering is a continuous process. This is because just as soon as you clutter, it keeps coming back, and you've got to deal with it regularly if you don't want to be buried under the mess. So this is by no means a one-

and-done task; it's an ongoing journey that shifts with the tides of your life. New responsibilities, unexpected curveballs, and evolving priorities all demand that you tweak your strategies, ensuring your mental clarity toolbox stays sharp and ready for action.

In college, you're juggling classes, a part-time job, and a social life that somehow requires some serious planning. Your go-to tricks might involve breaking tasks into bite-sized chunks or sneaking in power naps between study sessions. Fast forward to full-time adulting, and suddenly those techniques might feel as outdated as your account. Adapting is key. Every now and again, hit the mental "refresh" button and ask, "Is this still working for me?" Since life's curveballs don't wait, neither should your strategies. Staying flexible means you'll always have the right tool for the job.

And you can only achieve this through regular self-reflection. Self-reflection is your brain's wellness check-up. Since you wouldn't skip the doctor when something feels off (at least, you shouldn't), why ignore your mental health? Carve out time each week to ask yourself the big questions like, what's weighing you down? or are you saying 'yes' to too many things, like the overachiever you didn't ask to be?" Journaling can help. Think of it as free therapy, where you're both patient and the counselor. Scribble down your worries, triumphs, and to-do lists, then read it back like a script for a chaotic Netflix show. Patterns will emerge, and suddenly, you'll see what's adding clutter and what's clearing it away.

Let's talk about community support because decluttering your mind is way more fun with a hype squad. Whether it's a group of friends, a support group, or even your overly enthusiastic dog, having someone to share your journey with can make all the difference. Imagine swapping decluttering victories and fails, "I finally tackled my inbox, but now I'm drowning in unread notifications." These shared experiences spark new ideas and remind you that everyone's got their battles. Even better, sharing your story encourages others to open up, and together, you build a network of solidarity. As it turns out, mental decluttering is a team sport where everyone benefits when the bench is full.

Don't forget to celebrate your wins, no matter how small. Finally sorted your inbox? Break out the snacks. Managed five minutes of meditation without thinking about pizza? Victory dance! Recognizing these mini-achievements isn't just fun; it's fuel for the journey. Keep a "wins" journal to jot down every small triumph, turning it into a trophy cabinet of sorts for your brain. Over time, you'll see how far you've come, which always that feels amazing.

Adding a dazzle of humor into the mix would elevate your thought process. Laugh at the ridiculousness of some of your past worries. Celebrate progress with a hearty chuckle because laughter is the brain's way of saying, "You're doing great, buddy." Plus, it releases endorphins, a natural stress buster, and boosts your mood. When you can laugh at life's chaos, decluttering becomes less like a chore and more like an adventure. Invite your friend into the fun—maybe even turn it into a game. Who can tackle the most mental clutter before the pizza arrives?

Keeping your mind decluttered isn't about reaching a finish line. It's about staying in the race, reassessing your game plan, and celebrating every step. Flexibility keeps you resilient, self-reflection will act as your compass, and community provides the fuel. Toss in some laughter and small wins, and suddenly, this whole mental decluttering thing feels a lot less daunting and a whole lot more doable.

DAILY LAUGHS TO LIGHTEN YOUR LOAD

Finding the humor amid the chaos of life is like discovering an extra fry at the bottom of the bag. It's unexpected, but boy, does it make everything better. When the world feels like it's conspiring against you—coffee spills, missed buses, group project disasters—you may think of it as a scene from a slapstick comedy. Humor is like that friend who says, "You're fine, this is hilarious," and somehow, you believe them (Scott, 2020).

So, how do you harness this magical power of humor? The absurdity of it all is always a good place to start. Yes. That moment where you think you've had it up to neck level and can't take it anymore. That's your golden opportunity to laugh. Life has a knack for stacking ridiculousness in certain situations, and when you're mindful and light-hearted enough to spot the irony, it can help you smile instead of stress. It's a reminder that this moment, no matter how ridiculous, is just one scene in the epic blockbuster that is your life

But don't stop there. Consider building a humor routine—a daily dose of laughter, if you will. Watch a funny cat video while munching on cereal. Pop on a comedy podcast during your commute. Or end the day with a comic strip that leaves you chuckling before you hit the pillow. Think of it as mental floss, clearing out the gunk of stress and ensuring that, even in the worst of times, there's always a giggle lurking in your routine.

Routines provide structure, and a humor routine is like a reset button for your brain during stressful times. Imagine being in a total meltdown over an assignment. Suddenly, you recall that meme about a cat with a monocle and a caption that reads, "Indubitably." Instantly, your brain switches from spiraling panic to, "Okay, I can do this." Laughter is your secret weapon; a sneak attack on stress that leaves you smiling and ready to tackle the problem again (No Fooling: The Very Real Health Benefits of a (God) Prank or Joke, n.d.).

If laughing with yourself promises so many benefits, then laughing with others takes it up another level. Shared laughter is like group therapy, but with fewer tears and way more inside jokes. Think of all the times you've been with friends, giggling uncontrollably over something only half as funny as it seems. Those moments aren't just entertaining— they're bonding experiences that'll strengthen your relationships with these friends. So host a movie night, hit up a local comedy show, or just gather some friends for a bad-joke contest.

Laughter also enhances the level of empathy you feel on the way to becoming a better person. Inside jokes, shared chuckles, or even mutual groans over a failed group project remind us we're all in this mess together. Humor turns strangers into friends and friends into family. It's the ultimate icebreaker, and reminds you that at the end of the day, we're all in this together, and we've got this; and that's even when things look like they're falling apart (Scott, 2020).

The ability to diffuse conflict so neatly is perhaps another superpower of humor. Humor, when used wisely, acts as a pressure valve, reminding everyone that while the issue might be serious, a little levity can go a long way. At the same time, it is important to wield humor with care. Sure, a well-placed joke can defuse tension, but the wrong one can make things worse. Before cracking that joke, make sure to read the room, know your audience, and keep the humor kind. Ultimately, no one wants to feel like their "funny" comment turned into a cringe-worthy moment (No Fooling: The Very Real Health Benefits of a (Good) Prank or Joke, n.d.).

When you integrate humor into your life, it doesn't mean that you ignore problems or mask your genuine feelings. It's about giving yourself a different comic lens to navigate life's ups and downs. With humor, stress becomes a little less suffocating; connections with others become a little deeper, and even life's biggest challenges seem a little more manageable. So, laugh often, laugh loud, and remember: the universe might throw you curveballs, but you've got the humor to handle them.

THE NEVER-ENDING QUEST TO CLEAR YOUR MENTAL SPACE

To wrap up this chapter, remember that mental decluttering isn't a "one-and-done". You may think of it more like laundry. You take care of it, and it just keeps piling up. Life will keep tossing challenges your way, whether it's juggling classes, part-time jobs, or figuring out how to adult properly. The good news? You've got a toolkit now—prioritizing tasks, practicing mindfulness, journaling, setting boundaries, and indulging in self-care. These strategies come with a promise to help you slice through the clutter. Remember, as life changes, so must your approach. Stay flexible, and don't be afraid to ask yourself the big questions, like, "Why is my brain obsessing over that embarrassing thing I said three years ago?" or "Is there an easier way to handle this chaos?"

Above all, don't forget you're not in this alone. Your friends, family, and classmates are your support squad by default. Share your decluttering wins and fails with them. You'd be surprised with the advice (or at least the commiseration) they offer. Clear out your inbox. Meditate for five minutes without checking your phone. Those might seem small in the grand scheme of life goals you have planned out for yourself. But they remain wins! Celebrate them, no matter how small. Throw yourself a mini mental party. Add humor to the mix if you want; laughter is like a magic eraser for stress. From cracking innocent jokes with friends to laughing at how dramatic your brain gets sometimes, humor makes even the messiest parts of life a little more manageable.

On a final note, make sure to treat this whole decluttering thing like an epic quest of your own. Keep your mind open, your strategies flexible, and your sense of humor on standby. With a sprinkle of humor, a ton of adaptability, and the occasional mental kick up your backside to remind yourself that you've got this, you'll turn mental decluttering from a chore into an adventure worth celebrating.

Now, go forth and conquer your mental chaos. Just be minded that right when you think the clutter is gone for good, when the dust settles... it's in that moment you'll hear it. The faint rustle. The whisper of something... *returning.*

PART V: WRAP-UP

CHAPTER 11: STEPPING RIGHT INTO THE SHAMBLES!

Let's take a peek into the chaos carnival that, on most days, is our brain. Picture stepping into a space that should feel like a sanctuary, but rather feels like a room after a whirlwind. Thoughts and ideas scattered like open books; unfinished projects that end up forming gentle piles; and somewhere in the corner, there's probably a snack you forgot about. It all feels less like an organized, quiet library and more like a puzzle with pieces missing.

Now, if you're nodding along, you probably feel like its time to declare your independence, and you may want to read on. You see, mental clutter has a way of creeping on you. It sneaks up on you, first gradually, and then, all of a sudden.. By this time, you realize you're buried knee-deep under a mountain of random nonsense and wondering how you got here. And let's get real here: We've all been there.

In this chapter, which we've thoughtfully titled "Welcome to the Mind Maze" (because calling it "Your Journey to Mental Clarity" seemed a but too 'Zen' for what we're about to talk about), we'll dive headfirst into the world of mental clutter. It's a lot like untangling a ball of yarn, except the yarn is on fire, and the fire is your procrastination. But don't worry— you're not alone in this hot mess.

First, you'll learn why your brain sometimes feels overwhelmed, and we'll show you some proven, accessible strategies to help create order from this complexity. Somewhere along the way, we'll laugh at the absurdity of it all.

But eventually, we'll provide you with a clear path to everyday practices and techniques that will help you to navigate the mess.

Get ready—this chapter is here to help you cut through the chaos and bring some order to your mind. Think of it as tidying up your thoughts, with a bit of humor sprinkled in along the way.

THE "MESSY ROOM" METAPHOR

Our rooms present a worthy metaphor for how we interacts with our brains. Imagine stepping a room that looks like a tornado just held a talent show. Yesterday's clothes draped over every surface, random papers throwing a rave on the floor, and stuff you didn't even know you owned judging you silently from the corner. The chaos smacks you in the face, and then, what next? We stand at the door like a statue, because it feels like the only viable life choice. If this has ever happened to you at some point, then you should know that this is what mental clutter is in a nutshell. It's your brain stuffed to the brim with a lot of fluff, messy thoughts, half-finished tasks, and a kaleidoscope of shifting emotions.

The mess itself is not the problem; it's the emotional weight it places on your shoulders. You think, "Alright, time to handle this," but the sheer amount of chaos hits you like, *nope.* The same thing happens when your mind is a cluttered dumpster fire. You want to focus, you want to get stuff done, but your thoughts are doing gymnastics while you're stuck staring into the existential void.

Here's the thing: mental clutter doesn't just appear overnight (even if it feels that way). It's more like laundry—it sneaks up on you. A little procrastination here, an unresolved thought there, and boom! Before you know it, you're faced with enough chaos and internal unresolved drama that could rival a reality TV show. To make things worse, the stress of daily adulting, academic deadlines, or just keeping it together in a world full of group chats and TikTok trends may end up pushing you down the mental cliff.

But we already knew that these things, like death and taxes, are sure to happen. The question then becomes that how can we fix it? Let's borrow a move from professional organizers. When you walk into a messy room, you don't just clean the whole thing at once (unless you're secretly a wizard). You start small: one drawer, one corner, maybe just enough of the floor so you don't trip and eat carpet. Experts recommend breaking it down into bite-sized tasks to avoid that burnout spiral (The Clutter-Depression-Anxiety Cycle: How to Stop It, 2015).

Let's apply that same logic to your brain. Do this: Grab a notebook. Then, start dumping your thoughts onto paper. All of them. The good, the bad, and the "why am I even thinking about this?" thoughts. Now, once that's out of your head, you can start sorting out the clutter using the power of prioritization. Ask yourself: What needs attention right now? and what can I relegate to the back burner? The logic behind this methos is simple: Once you try to tackle everything at once, you risk crashing. No one cleaned up their room in 5 minutes. It's simply not happening. This is why you need to roll up your sleeves and actually go through the tedium and gradual process of sorting your mental clutter, else you end up crashing and having to start from scratch.

Routines are another hack that could speed up this process (of de-cluttering your brain) You may think of routines as your new BFFs. Having a morning routine keeps your house from becoming a war zone, right? The same goes for your brain. Having quick daily check-ins, be it journaling, meditating, or jotting down a to-do list, will keep you more decisive and in control of how your day pans out. We know this because very often, we tend to underestimate the impact that a time frame as little as 5 minutes can make all the difference in how your day turns out. (Lisa, 2020).

Here's the best part, decluttering your mind feels as magical as finding a random $20 in your coat pocket. You know that feeling when you finally clean a room and it's like hitting the reset button on life? A clear mind will do this for you. You'll have less noise, fewer distractions, and all of a sudden you now have space to focus on what truly matters.

And make no mistakes about it: The gist of decluttering isn't to be perfect. When you declutter, it's about finding peace in the chaos. Whether you're tidying up your room or your mental space, the goal is the same: creating room for joy, clarity, and a little less stress. So, go ahead. Tackle that mess (could be in your head or on your floor) that your future self will thank you for, and boy will you will be better for it!

UNTANGLING THE MENTAL MESS: WHAT'S IN YOUR HEAD?

Without even deciding to cosplay as a messy closet, life can get pretty chaotic. But sometimes, that's exactly what happens. Your thoughts morph into a giant pile of baggage, and suddenly the simplest decisions feel like you're trying to singlehandedly broker world peace. Like, why does picking a pizza topping have the same stress level as defusing a bomb? That's when you know your brain's officially in clutter overload.

If you've been there, then you know that mental clutter doesn't just chill quietly in the background. It shows up loud, unapologetically, and messy. takes the lead, dragging indecision and overthinking along for the ride. And so one minute you're trying to pick between pepperoni or mushrooms, the next you're rethinking your life choices. And let's not forget that feeling of being stuck. According to Rachel Jones, all these clutter can seriously send you into a frenzy and ruin your vibe. (The Clutter-Depression-Anxiety Cycle: How to Stop It, 2015).

Allowing though chaos to spiral out of control and dictate the pace of your life is where most of us get it wrong. So the question to ask is this: What we you do to eliminate mental mess and gather our thoughts in such a way that'll help us gain clarity on what to do to lead a fulfilled life? The first step is to perform a mental call-out, like "Hey brain, why are we overthinking a text from three days ago?" Taking stock of these personal micro and macro events can help. It's basically a 'vibe check' for your thoughts— what's stressing you out? Why does everything feel so chaotic? You can liken this to checking the weather: is it sunny with good vibes or thunderstorm-level chaos? Knowing what the weather is like can help you plan your day properly and regulate your emotions.

Now let's talk journaling. Journaling doesn't have to be some deep, soul-searching "Dear Diary" moment. It's as simple as just grabbing a pen and brain-dumping onto paper. Perhaps the cardinal rule of journaling is to write. Write it all down. If it comes to your mind, write it down – every cringe-worthy thought, every "Why did I say that?" moment, and every to-do that stresses you from merely thinking of it. One thing we tend to ignore is the psychological effect it brings. When we think about loved ones, days when we get to embark on a hobby, or enjoy memorable treats, and write them down, we tap into a rare opportunity to relive the joy of those experiences captured in the words we write. And it doesn't matter if it's in the present, past, or future. So, the question to ask yourself is this, does this thought spark joy? If no, then bye! If you don't get the gist, it's this: Journaling is cheap therapy. It gives you receipts for when you realize you've been spiraling about nothing.

And here's the twist—mental clutter doesn't just stay trapped in your head. Nope, it sneaks into your body too. Sudden headaches? Random fatigue even when you haven't moved a muscle? That's your body leaving little sticky notes that say, "Hey, can we sort out this mental mess?" Studies even suggest that having clutter, whether mental or physical, can impact your mood and overall satisfaction with life (Rogers & Hart, 2021).

The good news? You can totally fix it. Start small, like really small. Then, take five minutes to write down what's in your head. Alternatively, you could just sit and breathe (yes, that thing you're technically doing all the time. But now, with some intent). Think of it like you're tidying up one corner of your messy room. Follow a gradual, step-by-step process, because you know only little can be achieved when you try to tackle the whole disaster at once.

With time, these tiny steps start to add up. Your mental closet gets a little cleaner, your brain stops buffering, and suddenly you're the chill, thriving person you've always wanted to be. Okay, maybe not always , but you get the idea. Cluttered mind? Not today. You've got this.

STRESS MANAGEMENT 101: LAUGH IT AWAY

Sorting through mental clutter should be less about suffering and more about unlocking the hilarity hidden in chaos. Yes, you heard that right. The funny part. We all know that adulting is weird and stressful. But a the secret weapon that most of us don't know we have in tackling some of our daily challenges (yes, and that includes stressful, tense situations) is humor. Not just knock-knock jokes (though, to be fair, we won't judge), but the kind of laughter that makes you snort out loud and forget, for a moment, that your to-do list looks like a CVS receipt.

Laughter is the best medicine, or so they say. and it's not just because giggling burns calories (seriously, Google is your friend), there is a chemical reaction in the body to support this theory. When we laugh, our brain floods our system with endorphins (those magical feel-good chemicals that make you forget your problems) or at least make them seem a little less stressed. It also reduces cortisol (our stress hormone). So, the next time you're buried under a mountain of deadlines and existential dread, you may want to take a break for a hilarious meme or that one TikTok content creator that always cracks you up. Science says it's basically self-care (BioNeurix, 2022).

While a bit of humor is good, we would be mistaken to see it as just a stress reducer and nothing more. It can be a lifesaver as well. When your brain feels like a browser with 1,000 tabs open. Try to remember the last time your mind spiraled into chaos, and everything felt overwhelming, then something funny occurred (maybe you saw someone dressed in a way that you thought was plain hilarious, or you tripped in public and decided to own it with a dramatic bow—and suddenly, life didn't feel so impossible), now that's the power of humor. It won't wipe out your problems, but it sure makes it feel a lot less of a problem, so you feel a lot less miserable. When done correctly, it's one non-medical therapy that can suspend your negative feelings and enhance your mood for an extended period of time.

In all of these, let's not forget the magical bonding power of shared laughter. Nothing says "we're in this together" like cackling with your friends over an inside joke that no one else has a clue about. You could be in a chaotic group project or at a family gathering where Uncle Bob just told another dad joke, and then the laughter brings people closer. It's a social glue that acknowledges life's travails, but puts you in a position where you can demonstrate your gratitude to be alive by simply laughing it off" (County of Kern EAP | Anthem, 2023).

Humor does more than just help you survive awkward moments. It turns these memorable moments into stories that you'll remember and tell for years. Spilled coffee on yourself during a big presentation? Of course, it was gravely embarrassing. But believe it or not - one day you'll remember that day and laugh (or at least cringe less) about it. There's something uncanny about humor that helps you see life's bloopers as part of the reel, not the whole movie. It has the power to transform embarrassment into resilience and resilience into, well, a funny Instagram caption.

So, our message to you is to make humor part of your daily routine. And it's easier than you think. From binging a comedy show, to reading a funny book, or hanging out with friends who make you laugh so hard your abs hurt. (Bonus points for the calorie-burning), we can infuse humor into our daily experiences in the most creative ways. The best part? You don't have to fake joy or ignore serious stuff; just let humor poke holes in the heavy clouds when it can.

For college students buried under endless assignments and overpriced lattes, humor can be a lifesaver. Suddenly, that three-hour cram session becomes manageable when someone cracks a joke about mitochondria being the cell's "power plant" (and somehow it still makes you laugh). Even professors who sprinkle in a little humor notice students paying closer attention—because let's face it, who can resist a clever pun about quantum physics?

Workplaces are catching on the humor bug, too. They are now realizing that at work, laughter shouldn't just be for break rooms anymore; it should be a productivity hack to help workers recharge and 'go at it again' with a renewed vigor and positive attitude. When this happens, mangers are able to enhance creativity and get people brainstorming without fear of sounding ridiculous. After all, some of the most genius ideas that ever took off started with a sentence like, "I've got this crazy idea, but..."

So, how can you start reaping the benefits of humor in your life? Let these steps be your starting point:

- **Setting Humor Breaks:** Think coffee breaks, but funnier. Watch a quick comedy clip or scroll through your favorite memes.

- **A Humor Journal:** Keeping a humor journal close by makes it more convenient to write down funny highlights of your day or weird thoughts that made you laugh. This is an instant serotonin boost!

- **Joining Comedy Nights:** Whether it's open mic nights or improv classes, putting yourself in spaces that celebrate humor can be inspiring (and hilarious).

- **Trying Laughter Yoga:** You may not know this, but yes. Laughter yoga is a thing. It's kinda weird. But you'll be amazed how good it feels to just laugh for no reason.

Overall, life can be messy, unpredictable, or occasionally ridiculous. But when you let humor guide you through the clutter, you'll find the journey to be a lot less bumpy. Only then will it be a whole lot more fun to navigate this Mind Maze.

WRAPPING IT UP: INSIGHTS, GIGGLES, AND A PINCH OF SASS

Now as we wrap up this inquest into the delightful chaos that is mental clutter, it's important to understand one thing: The journey to understand our brain chaos can be like opening Pandora's box of self-awareness. We find out it's a space that overflows with sticky notes, forgotten to-do lists, and those viral TikToks we can't stop humming. When you start to unpeel these layers, you can find that it gets overwhelming at first. But once we start, we start to wonder why we didn't do it sooner.

To start with this task (sorting out the mental clutter) it may help to view your mind as a room where random tasks, feelings, and decisions have thrown the ultimate rager. The key to regaining control would be to break it all down into smaller, manageable pieces. Now, you don't 'Marie Kondo' the whole room in one go. At the same time, you don't have to organize your thoughts all at once either. The best approach then becomes to take it step by step, one scattered mental item at a time, and you'll start to see the floor—or at least, the metaphorical floor of your sanity.

If you're a young adult or college student, then life at that stage is basically one big juggling act with flaming swords. Young adults are thrown in for a loop, between academic pressures, social obligations, and the occasional existential crisis. When this happens, staying on top of things can feel impossible. This is where humor can be a useful tool of relief. It lightens the load, reminds you that you're not alone in the chaos, (Oh, and that it could be worse lol.) and helps you transform your overwhelming to-do list into something you can laugh about eventually.

Throwing in a healthy dose of humor and routine check-ins to your daily life isn't just about clearing the clutter. It's about adding that sparkle to the grind. It's like the neon sign in your mental cluttered room that says, "Hey buddy, don't take this too seriously." On worse days, it can offer that little-yet-crucial reminder you need that even the scariest tasks are survivable, especially if you can chuckle at how ridiculous they seem.

So this should be your plan: keep moving forward, taking one small step at a time. Let humor tag along for the ride. And sure, you might not declutter your entire mental landscape overnight, but we can assure you of one thing: Every little effort adds up. And who knows? With enough laughs and a bit of persistence, you might even start to enjoy the process. Or at least, you'll have some funny stories to tell when it's all said and done.

YOUR EXCLUSIVE ACCESS

Thank you so much for reading *Clear Your Mental Clutter*. I'm truly grateful for your time and support—it means the world to me!

If you'd like to continue this journey together, I'd love to stay connected. By joining my newsletter, you'll receive uplifting tips, practical insights, and early access to my upcoming books—straight to your inbox.

👉 Sign up here

https://theawesomereaders.com/

Or scan the QR Code below

Until next time,

Amelia Sagewood

REFERENCE LIST

BioNeurix. (2022). *What Is Emotional Self-Care and How Can You Benefit From It?* BioNeurix. https://bioneurix.com/blogs/blog/what-is-emotional-self-care? srsltid=AfmBOorpk9CPGlCE6jVywVyOezdSo5fUw OtFemrZoEzUEpg_pxDNdyUM Lisa. (2020, June 30). *How Less Clutter Makes Your Life Better When You're Overwhelmed by a Messy House* . This Simplified Home. https:// thissimplifiedhome.com/less-clutter/

Personal Growth - Articles - Emotional Wellness -County of Kern EAP | Anthem . (2023). Anthem EAP Program. https://www.anthemeap.com/ county-of-kern/emotional-wellness/personal-growth/articles

Rogers, C. J., & Hart, D. R. (2021, February). *Home and the extended-self: Exploring associations between clutter and wellbeing* . Journal of Environmental Psychology. https://doi.org/ 10.1016/j.jenvp.2021.101553

The Clutter-Depression-Anxiety Cycle: How to Stop It . (2015, May 26). Nourishing Minimalism. https://nourishingminimalism.com/clutter-depression-and-anxiety-a-vicious-cycle/

Hampton, K., Rainie, L., Lu, W., Shin, I., & Purcell, K. (2015, January 15). *Psychological Stress and Social Media Use* . Pew Research Center: Internet, Science & Tech. https://www.pewresearch.org/ internet/2015/01/15/psychological-stress-and-social-media-use-2/

Kyron, M. J., Rees, C. S., Lawrence, D., Carleton, R. N., & McEvoy, P. M. (2021, February). *Prospective risk and protective factors for psychopathology and wellbeing in civilian emergency services personnel: a systematic review* . Journal of Affective Disorders. https://doi.org/10.1016/j.jad. 2020.12.021

Negative self-talk: 8 ways to quiet your inner critic . (2023, October 3). Calm Blog. https:// www.calm.com/blog/negative-self-talk

The Clutter-Depression-Anxiety Cycle: How to Stop It . (2015, May 26). Nourishing Minimalism. https://nourishingminimalism.com/clutter-depression-and-anxiety-a-vicious-cycle/

The Impact Of Social Media On Mental Health | PepTalk . (2024). PepTalk. https:// www.getapeptalk.com/journal/the-impact-of-social-media-on-mental-health

Weigelt, O., Seidel, J. C., Erber, L., Wendsche, J., Varol, Y. Z., Weiher, G. M., Gierer, P., Sciannimanica, C., Janzen, R., & Syrek, C. J. (2023, February 17). *Too Committed to Switch Off— Capturing and Organizing the Full Range of Work-Related Rumination from Detachment to Overcommitment* . International Journal of Environmental Research and Public Health. https://doi.org/10.3390/ijerph20043573

5 simple ways to practice mindfulness in daily life . (n.d.). Calm Blog. https://www.calm.com/blog/5-simple-ways-to-practice-mindfulness-in-daily-life

Alam, M. A. (2024, November 8). *Living with Less: The Benefits of Minimalism for Mental Clarity* . Medium; ILLUMINATION. https://medium.com/ illumination/living-with-less-the-benefits-of-minimalism-for-mental-clarity-63947e5283bb

Astoul, E. (2023, January 25). *Mental Minimalism: Brilliant Tips To Declutter Your Mind* . Green with Less. https://greenwithless.com/declutter-your-mind-mental-minimalism/

Hoshaw, C. (2022, March 29). *What is mindfulness? A simple practice for greater wellbeing* . Healthline. https:// www.healthline.com/health/mind-body/what-is-mindfulness

Murphy, A. (2024, October 14). *100+ Scientific Benefits of Meditation* . Declutterthemind.com; Declutter The Mind. https:// declutterthemind.com/blog/100-scientific-benefits-of-meditation

Pal, P., Hauck, C., Goldstein, E., Bobinet, K., & Bradley, C. (2018, December 13). *5 simple mindfulness practices for daily life* . Mindful. https://www.mindful.org/take-a-mindful-

moment-5-simple-practices-for-daily-life/ *10+ Scientifically Proven Ways Laughter Can Relieve Stress* . (2019, November). University of St.

Augustine for Health Sciences. https:// www.usa.edu/blog/how-laughter-can-relieve-stress/

Haupt, A. (2023, May 8). *8 Ways to Find Humor in Your Everyday Life* . Time. https://time.com/ 6273110/humor-health-benefits-strategies/

Mayo Clinic Staff. (2023, September 22). *Stress relief from laughter? It's no joke* . Mayo Clinic. https://www.mayoclinic.org/healthy-lifestyle/ stress-management/in-depth/stress-relief/

art-20044456

More, I. (2024, May 2). *Abundance Therapy Center* . Abundance Therapy Center. https:// www.abundancetherapycenter.com/blog/ incorporating-more-laughter-into-your-life

Why Laughter Is The Best Medicine For Your Whole Health . (2024, March 19). College of Public Health. https://www.unthsc.edu/college-of-public-health/why-laughter-is-the-best-medicine-for-

your-whole-health/

Yim, J. (2016, July 1). *Therapeutic benefits of laughter in mental health: A theoretical review* . The Tohoku Journal of Experimental Medicine. https://pubmed.ncbi.nlm.nih.gov/27439375/

9 Benefits of Time Management Success Stories for Employees . (2024, November 26). Week Plan.

https://weekplan.net/time-management-success-stories

Asana. (2024, January 29). *The Eisenhower matrix: How to prioritize your to-do list* . Asana. https://asana.com/resources/eisenhower-matrix

Elder, H. (2024). *SMART goal setting in Tustin: Tips from Tustin Cadillac* . Retrieved from https:// www.tustincadillac.com/mastering-goal-setting-and-achievement-strategies-for-success-in-tustin/

Perks:, B. (2024). *Beyond Perks: Real-World Wellness Initiatives That Work* . Hackinghrlab.io. https://hackinghrlab.io/blogs/holistic-wellness-success-stories/

Setting. (2024). *Setting Priorities - FasterCapital* . FasterCapital. https://fastercapital.com/startup-topic/Setting-Priorities.html

Scroggs, L. (2021). *The Eisenhower Matrix* . Todoist. https://todoist.com/productivity-methods/eisenhower-matrix

Bay. (2024, May 6). *5 Effective Strategies to Overcome Perfectionism* . Bay Area CBT Center. https://bayareacbtcenter.com/overcome-perfectionism/

How To Overcome Perfectionism: Embrace Imperfection & Reduce Stress . (2024, November 4). Mental Health Center of San Diego. https:// mhcsandiego.com/blog/how-to-overcome-perfectionism/

Nazari, N. (2022, May 16). *Perfectionism and Mental Health problems: Limitations and Directions for Future Research* . World Journal of Clinical Cases. https://doi.org/10.12998/ wjcc.v10.i14.4709

Sandoiu, A. (2018, October 12). *How perfectionism affects your (mental) health* . Www.medicalnewstoday.com. https:// www.medicalnewstoday.com/articles/323323

Vijeth, A. (2023, December 2). *Living Authentically: Embracing Vulnerability for Meaningful Connections* . Medium. https:// medium.com/@arjunvijeth/living-authentically-embracing-vulnerability-for-meaningful-connections-45f3a3e291ea

mperryLCSW. (2023, July 17). *The Power of Emotional Vulnerability: Embracing Authenticity and Connection* . Margaret Perry, LCSW. https:// perrymhs.com/emotional-vulnerability/

Batuhan Odabaş. (2024, November 15). *Multitasking is a Lie: Here's What You Should Do Instead* . Medium; Tech Encyclopedia. https://

medium.com/tech-encyclopedia/multitasking-is-a-   lie-heres-what-you-should-do-instead-a4372e1efec3

Health, M. (2024, April 8). *Digital Detox: Reducing Screen Time for Mental Well-being* . Michigan Health and Wellness Center. https://michiganhealthandwellness.com/digital-detox-reducing-screen-time-for-mental-well-being/

Keer, L. (2023, September 27). *Digital Distraction and Its Impact on Your Health* . Massachusetts General Hospital. https://www.massgeneral.org/news/article/digital-distraction-and-its-impact-on-your-health

Why Multitasking is a Myth and How to Truly Be Eficient . (2024). Mogul AI. https://onmogul.com/   posts/why-multitasking-is-a-myth-and-how-to-truly-be-eficient

What is Digital Distraction? Causes, Impacts & How to Avoid It? (2024, November 25). KrispCall. https://krispcall.com/blog/digital-distraction/

wwintern. (2024, July 18). *Digital Detox: Managing Screen Time for Better Mental Health -DFD Russell Medical Centers* . DFD Russell Medical   Centers. https://www.dfdrussell.org/   digital-detox-managing-screen-time-for-better-mental-health/

Chowdhury, M. R. (2019, April 9). *The Neuroscience of Gratitude and Effects on the Brain* . PositivePsychology.com.   https://positivepsychology.com/neuroscience-of-gratitude/

Komase, Y., Watanabe, K., Hori, D., Nozawa, K., Hidaka, Y., Iida, M., Imamura, K., & Kawakami, N. (2021, January). *Effects of gratitude intervention on mental health and well-being among workers: A systematic review* . Journal of Occupational Health. https://doi.org/10.1002/1348-9585.12290

Nevin, A. S. (2024, May 15). *Single-Tasking* . Single-Tasking. https://centerforbrainhealth.org/ article/single-tasking

Staff, 7GM. (2023, August 19). *Master Your Day: Harnessing the Power of Daily Routines for a Successful Life* . 7 Good Minutes; 7 Good Minutes.

https://7goodminutes.com/master-your-day-harnessing-the-power-of-daily-routines-for-a-successful-life/

Tepliczky, P. (2024). *The road to wellness: Building your best daily routine* . *Wellis Spa Blog* . Retrieved from https://wellisspa.com/blog/best-daily-routine/

https://www.facebook.com/verywell. (2021). *How Single-Tasking Can Reduce the Stress in Your Life* . Verywell Mind. https://www.verywellmind.com/ single-tasking-for-productivity-and-stress-management-3144753

Desai , D., Momin, A., Hirpara, P., Jha, H., Thaker, R., & Patel, J. (2024). *Exploring the Role of Circadian Rhythms in Sleep and Recovery: A Review Article* . Cureus. https://doi.org/10.7759/ cureus.61568

Exercise and Mental Health: 8 Benefits for Your Mood . (2024). Hingehealth. https:// www.hingehealth.com/resources/articles/exercise-and-mental-health/

Gómez-Pinilla, F. (2008, July). *Brain foods: the effects of nutrients on brain function* . Nature Reviews Neuroscience. https://doi.org/10.1038/ nrn2421

Selhub, E. (2022, September 18). *Nutritional psychiatry: Your brain on food *. Harvard Health Blog; Harvard Health Publishing. https:// www.health.harvard.edu/blog/nutritional-psychiatry-your-brain-on-food-201511168626

Suni, E., & Dimitriu, A. (2024, March 26). *Mental health and sleep* . Sleep Foundation. https:// www.sleepfoundation.org/mental-health

kingry, madeline. (2024, June 3). *Exploring the Mind-Body Connection: Exercise and Mental Health* . SCA Health | Insights. https:// insights.sca.health/insight/article/exploring-the-mind-body-connection-exercise-and-mental-health

Coaching, D. L. (2024). *Setting Yourself Up for Small Wins* . Theselftrustcoach.com. https:// www.theselftrustcoach.com/blog/small-wins

Henderson, S. (2015, March 31). *Laughter and Learning: Humor Boosts Retention* . Edutopia; George Lucas Educational Foundation. https://www.edutopia.org/blog/laughter-learning-humor-boosts-retention-sarah-henderson

Moeinian, S. (2024, May 31). *How Does Humor Play a Role in Mental Health and Wellness* . Rivia Mind. https://riviamind.com/how-does-humor-play-a-role-in-mental-health-and-wellness/

No Fooling: The Very Real Health Benefits of a (Good) Prank or Joke . (n.d.). Cleveland Clinic. https://health.clevelandclinic.org/benefits-of-joking

Overcoming Self-Imposed Barriers to Success . (2024). Becomebraveenough.com. https://www.becomebraveenough.com/blog/overcoming-self-imposed-barriers-to-success

Scott, E. (2020, October 25). *How to Find the Humor in Stressful Situations* . Verywell Mind. https://www.verywellmind.com/laughter-as-a-coping-mechanism-3144664

www.ingramcontent.com/pod-product-compliance
Lightning Source LLC
Chambersburg PA
CBHW071332130626
46556CB00004B/1858